Letters of Ascent

Letters of Ascent

Spiritual Direction in the Letters of Bernard of Clairvaux

Michael C. Voigts

James Clarke & Co

for Sheryl, Daniel, and Julianne

James Clarke & Co
P.O. Box 60
Cambridge
CB1 2NT
United Kingdom

www.jamesclarke.co
publishing@jamesclarke.co

ISBN: 978 0 227 17441 8

British Library Cataloguing in Publication Data
A record is available from the British Library

First published by James Clarke & Co, 2014

Copyright © Michael C. Voigts, 2013

Published by arrangement
with Pickwick Publications

Contents

Acknowledgments

THIS WORK WOULD NOT have been possible without the cooperation and spiritual direction of several people who have guided my life and work.

In March of 1992, Professor Jerry L. Mercer at Asbury Theological Seminary introduced me to the writings of a twelfth-century monk named Bernard. That event began a spiritual and historical journey that continues to this day. I am forever grateful for Jerry's presence in my life. For his interest in and assistance with finding obscure and ancient resources, I hold a debt of gratitude to the late Fr. Chrysogonus Waddell of Gethsemani Abbey, whose smile and intelligent wit will forever remain with me. I'm also thankful for the scholarship and gentle wisdom of J. Steven O'Malley, without whom this project could not have been completed. For their love, encouragement, and acceptance of my presence, I wish to express my appreciation to the Lay Cistercians of Gethsemani Abbey. As for family, Sheryl, Daniel, and Julianne, this project could not have been completed without their love, patience, and support. They continue to encourage me by pretending that they are as interested in Bernard of Clairvaux as I am! Above all, I am thankful to God for entrusting me with this work.

CHAPTER 1

Bernard of Clairvaux in the Twelfth-Century World

SPIRITUAL DIRECTION INVOLVES TWO willing participants: a director and a person or persons being directed. It happens more in the reality of life than in esoteric statements in books worth quoting from generation to generation. To understand Bernard of Clairvaux as a spiritual director, a basic understanding of the real Bernard set in time and culture is necessary. Modern readers have very little in common with medieval Europeans; their language, worldview, culture, politics, and economics are foreign to us. Other than an understanding of God, we share with medievals only our human identity. To set in context the spiritual direction Bernard offers in his letters, we must first explore Bernard in the twelfth-century European world.

BERNARD AS A CHILD OF THE CHURCH

Some individuals are born before their time. These unique people find themselves in a culture unprepared for their ideas, technological or scientific insights, or philosophical theories. Peter Abelard, the twelfth-century philosopher and theologian, was one of these people. Peter's contemporary, Bernard of Clairvaux, was not. Bernard de Fontaines (1090–1153) entered a Europe and an ecclesiastical system perfectly suited for him.[1] The Roman church was flourishing, medieval European culture was entering the high point in its history, and scholasticism had begun to have its own place in

1. Storrs, *Bernard of Clairvaux*, 72.

theological debates. This medieval renaissance did not arrive without tension, however, but was full of controversy and occasional violence.

Under the Gregorian Reform of the eleventh century, monasticism was ripe for renewal. The establishment by Pope Gregory VII of an overarching papal control structure for the church was based, in part, on a supposed rediscovery of the *Donation of Constantine*, a document purported to demonstrate that a centralized papal authority was an ancient tradition. This centralized power transformed the role of the pope from that of a delegating authority to a ruler involved in the many details of governing a multinational society. While the Gregorian popes enjoyed this new dominance in worldly affairs, it did not come without a price. They now had to endure the daily traffic and long speeches of litigants who each believed their issue was of the utmost importance. As R. W. Southern states, the popes became prisoners of their own machine.[2] Gregory wanted more centralized control, and he received it, along with the detailed and miniscule litigation that came with it. Nevertheless, the benefits of papal control outweighed the administrative frustrations. For example, the threat of excommunication was, in these early years of reform, a powerful political tool in a highly superstitious society, as in the excommunication of King Henry IV of Germany.[3] Nearly everyone, from the religious to the peasantry, feared the wrath of God in the world to come. Since the clerics wielded control over laity by claiming to be God's representatives on earth, church leaders wielded considerable power, forcing both king and layperson alike into submission in order to garnish God's good favor. This supposed freedom from the secular authorities gave the church the enviable position of becoming the dominant force in society as a whole.

European medieval culture lagged behind Byzantium in orderliness, sophistication, and administrative structure. In the East, a unified currency, salaried administrative rulers, and centralized justice provided a greater stability than the Western culture of military allegiances and power, fluctuating church support, and multi-nationalism. Visitors to Constantinople often commented on the dazzling decorative displays of the courts and dress of the rulers. In Europe, the strength of one's army or number of serfs, not one's opulence, demonstrated power and authority. Not until

2. Southern, *Western Society and the Church in the Middle Ages*, 110.

3. Henry, apparently testing Pope Gregory's resolve, appointed bishops to three sees in Italy, which Gregory claimed as his own. At the Diet of Worms in 1076, Henry withdrew himself from the obedience of Rome and was excommunicated. The results were disastrous for the German king.

European exploration of Byzantium, particularly during the Crusading period, did the nobility of Europe focus their efforts on ornate décor in dress and architecture.

The tenth and eleventh centuries were periods of political maneuvering throughout Europe. In France, the great fiefs of Normandy, Brittany, Flanders, and Burgundy began to take shape, joining Aquitaine as independent nations with their own distinct cultures and customs. These feudal states, ruled by powerful families, became larger and more powerful through strategic political alliances, marriages, and military conquests. In 1066, Normandy became the most powerful state when Duke William added England to his land possessions. In the Holy Roman Empire kings found it difficult to keep order and peace within the kingdom and to keep the pagan nations to the north and east at bay.

This period in the history of the West was an age of experimentation, tolerance, monastic expansion, and enterprise. It has also been called one of the most significant periods both socially and theologically in the history of Christianity.[4] Monastic expansion in spirituality, politics, and finance fueled an already expanding economy. This monastic growth was supported by secular society, as benefactors gave their lands for the development of new monasteries. These donors desired the cultivation, safekeeping, and management of their lands that monastic foundations offered, and the prayers of the monks on behalf of their patrons offered a sense of eternal security.

Western Europe was experiencing for the first time a significant growth of cities, commerce, and the development of the burghers. Cistercian monastic establishments on the frontiers of Europe expanded useable lands and territories, opening new areas for civilization. The acceptance of profit-making ushered a new understanding of trade to the medieval world. Monasticism, too, was experiencing the benefits of the accumulation of wealth. The issues of capital, expansion, and commerce became a focus in all strata of society. Western Europe in the early twelfth century was in many ways the pinnacle of the medieval West. Some have even referred to this prosperity and interest in new ideas the so-called "twelfth-century renaissance."[5]

4. Constable, *The Reformation of the Twelfth Century*, 5.

5. Recent interest in identifying a twelfth-century Renaissance began with Charles Haskins' 1927 work *The Renaissance of the Twelfth Century*.

Not since the days of Charlemagne had Europe been as politically or financially stable as in the early twelfth century. Great conquesting campaigns were over, and the nobility, peasants, and ecclesiastical leaders desired to take advantage of the expanding economic growth of the period. Despite the positive aspects of this growth and expansion of Europe, however, both the church and temporal society needed restraint and spiritual grounding. They found these qualities in Bernard of Clairvaux.

Most scholars place his birth in 1090 at his father's estate in Burgundy, a beautiful chateau on a hill overlooking the city of Dijon. He was the middle child in a family of seven children. From all accounts, his parents lived a pious life, faithful to the church. According to the *Vita Prima*, his father, Tescelin, came from a long established military family. Although Tescelin was a respected member of the lower nobility throughout Burgundy, most of Bernard's later political connections seemed to come from the family of his mother, Aleth. Although his brothers seemed to delight in training for a knightly occupation like their father, Bernard was more comfortable with books and clearly had a deep affection for his mother. From all accounts, her death, when Bernard was a teenager, had a profound influence on his life.

The story of Bernard, along with thirty members of his family and extended relatives, bypassing the respectable and comfortable Cluny for the struggling and austere Citeaux is well known. How Bernard was able to inspire the others to join him at Citeaux is an example of this man's will and charisma. Overlooking the city of Dijon, the family's hilltop home provided security and twelfth-century comfort for young Bernard and his family. That his brothers and he were expected to assume their places in society was no obstacle to the young nobleman. By his pure will and passion, and through his recruiting of others to join him at Citeaux, Bernard demonstrated his ability to inspire others to abandon their personal desires for his agenda. Already at an early age, Bernard was well aware of this personal charism, and he knew how to use it.[6]

Some have described Bernard as a tall, skeletal person with light golden hair and a reddish beard. He had a peaceful intensity about him that caused others, even those who opposed him, to pause in awe when he entered a room. He also suffered from severe physical maladies from his

---

6. Leclercq, "Towards a Sociological Interpretation," 21.

youth, including headaches and digestive disorders, which regressed to a point at which he could scarcely eat anything at all.[7]

THE ZEAL FOR REFORM

Whether or not Citeaux would have closed had not Bernard and his companions arrived is an open question. We know that before the Burgundians arrived Abbot Stephen Harding and the others had questioned their future. The fledgling Cistercian Order began in 1098 as an attempt to regain strict interpretation of both the order and discipline of Benedict's monastic *Rule*. Their harsh lifestyle and lack of sophisticated accommodations caused several of these reforming monks to succumb to illness and starvation. Some evidence exists that the arrival of Bernard with his band of men to Citeaux did not save the monastery from extinction but provided the means for the Cistercians to expand to new foundations.[8] Regardless of the situation, the revitalization of Citeaux with the admission of the new converts provided Stephen with a healthy opportunity to expand the small order in 1113.

Stephen, impressed by both the determination of the young Bernard to live a life in complete submission to the rule and with his natural leadership abilities, asked Bernard to found a monastery in a region to the north of Citeaux in 1115. Bernard's choice for a location was in the remote Absinthe Valley. Clairvaux would serve as the only monastery Bernard would ever oversee and become the mother of dozens of daughter houses. At the time of Bernard's death, the community at Clairvaux numbered more than seven hundred. Some have argued that the sole reason of the success of Clairvaux was the activity of Bernard himself.[9] Certainly Bernard's very presence and nature had a significant effect on the growth of Clairvaux and the entire order. Yet, Bernard believed that his charisma only served as the means to motivate people to seek a significance for their lives that was far deeper than even the movement of Cistercian monasticism.

7. *Ep* 310; *SBOp* 8:230.
8. Mahn, *L'Ordre cistercien*, 60–61.
9. McCaffrey "The Basics of Monastic Living in St. Bernard," 157–62.

THE CISTERCIAN IDEAL

The Cistercians were not the only new orders in twelfth-century Europe. They were part of a broader movement of reform that included the Carthusians, Savigniacs, Grandmontines, and Premonstrantensians. The rise of wandering preachers, hermits, and recluses also gained popularity during this era. Any successful reform movement needs a leader who has both a charismatic personality and a disciplinarian spirit. Bernard seems to have possessed both.[10] What set the Cistercians apart from other reforming monastic movements were their high ideals, strong administrative control (a particular gift of Cistercian founder Stephen Harding), and the person of Bernard himself.

For Bernard, the mystical union between Christ and the church exists to the extent that the two cannot exist without one another. Because Christians are united to Christ through the church, this mystical marriage is not for their own good but for the good of others. As Jean Leclercq states, Bernard understood Christians as "united to all, called on to watch over all, and consequently responsible for all."[11] Although people lived in communities—whether abbeys, cities, or rural villages—their true citizenship was in heaven, and people in all areas of life should strive to live in such a manner as to reflect this citizenship, as the church is the divine norm of national identity.[12]

The early Order of Citeaux desired to live as a faithful spouse by carefully following St. Benedict's *Rule*. The Cistercians' emphasis on poverty, asceticism, simplicity in art and architecture, and ordinary lifestyle was a mere function of their devotion to Christ. Breaking from traditional monastic customs, the Cistercians set themselves apart from other orders (even the new orders). They were obsessed with the *puritas Regulae* and desired none other than to follow Christ through a judicious following of its text. Bernard seems to have focused on particular aspects of the Rule that he believed provided the means for real union with Christ and differentiated these aspects of the Rule from what he deemed as secondary elements, which he rarely mentioned in his writings.[13]

10. Constable, *Reformation of the Twelfth Century*, 112.

11. Leclercq, "Saint Bernard of Clairvaux and the Contemplative Community," 97–112.

12. Williams, "The Political Philosophy of Saint Bernard of Clairvaux," 466–69.

13. Leclercq, "St. Bernard in Our Times," 16.

Of course, this focus on the means for following Christ made an implicit commentary on other monastic orders that had a more open understanding of Benedict. For the early Cistercians, the monastery, more than a school of learning, was a school of charity.[14] This understanding caused many to view the Cistercians as pious, prideful monks who only knew humility in the context of comparing themselves to others.

ECCLESIASTICAL ACTIVITY

For an individual who had fled the world, Bernard spent a considerable amount of time in it. Yet, for all of his activities outside of Clairvaux, Bernard's complex personality made him a polarizing figure. Emotions controlled his actions and he was known to be compulsive. By using the right terms and choice of words others could easily draw him into situations that had nothing to do with him or the Cistercian Order. William of St. Thierry, for example, knew he could draw Bernard into the Abelard affair by eloquently portraying the scholar in a letter to the saint as a perverter of the "belief in the Trinity, of the person of the Mediator, and of the mystery of our Redemption."[15] After reading William's pamphlet on Abelard (and seemingly not checking the facts himself), Bernard thrust himself into the controversy, calling for Abelard's condemnation. It should be noted, however, that in his response letter to William, Bernard acknowledges, "I am not in the habit of trusting my judgments, especially in such grave matters as these."[16] Nevertheless, this admission did not prevent Bernard from pursuing the condemnation of Abelard's writings at the Council of Sens in 1139.

While Bernard's use of letters as means for involving himself in the affairs of the world was extensive, some have questioned the effectiveness of Bernard's ecclesiastical activity. Many of his letters have a spontaneously sour flavor about them, causing the reader to have pity on the poor scribe that took Bernard's dictation. Yet, the success of these letter-writing campaigns was not always clear. For example, during the papal schism of the 1130s, Bernard wrote vociferously in support of Innocent II. Following the condemnation of Anacletus, Bernard used his apparent political favor with Innocent to write more than fifty letters to the pontiff. Conversely, Innocent

14. Bamberger, "The Monastic Vision of Saint Bernard of Clairvaux," 46–58.

15. *Disp. adv. Petrum Abelardum*, PL 180.249–282..

16. *Ep* 327; *SBOp* 8:263.

apparently wrote only five letters to Bernard, three of which were co-addressed to both Bernard and a bishop. In this instance, the letter-writing activity seems only to have been unidirectional. A more accurate interpretation of Bernard's effectiveness, however, is not whether or not the pontiff replied to the saint, but whether or not Innocent acted on Bernard's desires.

EARLY ECCLESIASTICAL INTERVENTIONS

In its early years, as the foundation of Clairvaux continued to gain converts and financial support, Bernard experienced his first two activities outside of the Cistercian world. Coincidentally, both of these activities regarded Cluny, the formidable and prosperous Benedictine Abbey and Burgundian neighbor of Clairvaux to the south. The first major exchange between Bernard and Cluny regarded the situation in the autumn of 1116 with Bernard's nephew Robert, a Cistercian monk, and coincided with the period in which the young, sickly abbot was secluded from his monks.

During Bernard's confinement Robert, seemingly growing weary of the Cistercian ideal—and taking advantage of the situation of Bernard's isolation from the community—arranged to be taken to Cluny and subsequently was given nearly royal treatment by the Cluniacs. The young abbot of Clairvaux handled the situation very differently than an older and more confident Bernard might have handled it. He understood his lowly political position compared to powerful Cluny. More importantly, he knew that Robert's parents had promised him to Cluny in the child's youth. In a later reflection Bernard recorded that Robert left "*me invito.*"[17] Other than Bernard's revealing and emotional letter to Robert, written a few years after his departure, and a second mention of the situation in the letter cited above to Jorannus, Abbot of St. Nicasius of Rheims, Bernard remained overtly silent on this matter, at least publicly.

The second early incident, also with Cluny, occurred at the instigation of Bernard's new friend, William of St. Thierry, who asked Bernard to compose a document on the excesses and laxities within the current state of monasticism. It resulted in the publication of the *Apologia* in the 1120s. Whether satirical or not, the emergence of this document established Bernard as a vocal young reformer who was not timid about promoting reform outside his own Order. The strained relationship between the Cistercians

17. *Ep* 32; *SBOp* 7:87.

and the Cluniacs was exaggerated, to say the least, by the publication of this manuscript.

The *Apologia* has been misunderstood since its first appearance. Rather than a scathing attack on the practices of Cluny, Bernard begins by criticizing his own Cistercian monks for spiritual pride. Bernard's use of sarcasm and irony is masterful. One must remember, however, that Bernard did not criticize Cluny for Cluny's sake. The famous abbey is mentioned only rarely in the corpus of the text. Bernard had respect for them and their place in the monastic community. For Bernard, both Cluny and Clairvaux could co-exist peacefully and faithfully in the same church, stating, "It is not our Order alone, nor yours alone that makes up this unity, but ours and yours together."[18] Bernard understood the various orders in the church as the many different jeweled adornments worn by the spouse of Christ. For him, each had its own place and special significance to Christ, the church's bridegroom.

The Papal Schism of 1130

These small skirmishes with the Cluniacs were of minor consequence compared to Bernard's first major ecclesiastical engagement that placed him at the center of the European political world. Before 1130 Bernard's involvement in the affairs of others had been limited to settling disputes between individuals, arguments over land between nobles and the Crown, and in other small matters. His involvement seems to have been behind the scenes, away from public attention. This was about to change, as Bernard's involvement in the papal schism would cause his reputation and fame to move from Burgundy to all of Europe.

As Pope Honorarius II lay near death, a member of the Curia, Haimeric, Chancellor of the Holy See, was aware of the papal ambitions of Peter Leonis. Leonis, a cardinal, had once been a monk at Cluny. Apparently, Leonis was not known for his virtuous life, and very few individuals had positive remarks about his character. Born into a wealthy family, he spent most of his career focusing on the accumulation of riches as he progressed politically through the ecclesiastical ranks. Both Peter the Venerable of Cluny and Suger of St. Denis questioned the character of Leonis, even though they mutually had an affiliation with him and understood his great political power.

18. *Apo* 4.7; *SBOp* 3:87.

In order to spare the church from the ascension of Leonis to the Holy See, Haimeric and others moved the ailing Honorarius to a remote location to hide his impending death. Upon his death, but before the public announcement and post-burial hiatus, Haimeric, four cardinal bishops, five cardinal priests, and four cardinal deacons met and elected Gregory of San Angelo as Pope Innocent II.

Rumors of the death of Honorarius spread to Peter Leonis and his cardinal supporters, who outnumbered the cardinals who supported Gregory. They unanimously elected Leonis as Pope Anacletus II. Clearly, these cardinals followed the regulations more exactly, as they waited the prescribed number of days to hold the election. The supporters of Innocent II, however, felt they needed to act boldly to spare the church the scandal of Peter Leonis. Anacletus had a majority support of the Roman people and the political operatives within the church. Innocent had the support of the church's reformers. Something had to be done, and King Louis *"le gros"* of France took the initiative. Although he was a friend of Anacletus, he nonetheless summoned a council in Etampes of the chief ecclesiastical leaders in his realm to decide the matter, and he personally invited Bernard to attend. Bernard clearly supported Innocent II as Bernard believed his character was much more becoming of a pope than the ambitious, wealthy Anacletus.

As Bernard left Clairvaux for Etampes, he was leaving behind a life of relative seclusion, embarking upon a new epoch in his life. In fact, this may be the second, major turning point in Bernard's life (the first is when he left a secular career for Citeaux).[19] At this council, Bernard's influence in Europe began to be felt. According to the hagiographical account of Bernard's life, the *Vita Prima*, the members of the council waited for Bernard's arrival before conducting any business and unanimously appointed Bernard to be their spokesperson. In fact, the *Vita Prima* states that when Bernard made his public decision to support Innocent, all in attendance at the council agreed with him unanimously and with enthusiasm.

Bernard was now the spokesperson of France in the papal schism, and he spent a considerable amount of time and energy supporting the claim of Innocent II. The task was considerable, taking into account the fact that Anacletus had more political clout than Innocent and had connections and support across the continent, including France and England, but particularly in Italy. Whether intentional or not, Bernard's activities during this papal division had the effect of establishing Bernard as the moral authority of

19. James, *Saint Bernard of Clairvaux*, 105.

Europe. He accomplished this not by skirting the powers of the church but by using the very political and bureaucratic structures within the church for his own reforming purposes.

Bernard's persistence continued, and after eight years of schism, the supporters of Anacletus submitted to Innocent at the death of the anti-pope, who died, according to the *Vita Prima*, "losing heart," as he knew that his supporters were defecting to Innocent. Interestingly, Bernard disagreed with the victorious Innocent II in how to deal with these detractors. The pope desired a public and formal submission by them. Bernard, conversely, believed their capitulation should be handled in private, and with grace.[20]

Bernard's frequent travels and correspondence with much of the European church during these tumultuous eight years gave him a considerable reputation—and respect—even among those who did not support Innocent's papal claim. He returned to Clairvaux exhausted, but found himself being called periodically by Innocent II to intervene in political skirmishes, particularly in France. It seemed the entire world knew of this abbot. For the remainder of his life, Bernard would use this popularity to his advantage, sometimes more successfully than others.

ABELARD

The controversy regarding Peter Abelard may be Bernard's most embarrassing ecclesiastical involvement. It began with William of St. Thierry, Bernard's trusted friend, who in a letter to the saint, warned of the doctrine of Peter Abelard. Apparently, Bernard knew little of Abelard's erroneous teaching yet seemingly without hesitation began a campaign to have the teachings of Abelard condemned.[21] In 1139 the Council of Sens ensued, and like the Apostle Paul before Festus in Caesarea, Abelard utilized his political rights and appealed to Rome. As Abelard raced to Rome to defend himself, he was told at Cluny that his books had already been burned. His academic career over and his reputation tarnished, Abelard retired as a monk at Cluny.

Possibly the greatest academic mind of his time, Peter Abelard gained a reputation for challenging established teachings and doctrines, based on a modified form of nominalism in which he cast doubt on traditional Christian formulations. He gained fame as an eloquent and persuasive teacher

20. Dumesnil, *Saint Bernard*, 82.
21. *Ep* 327; *SBOp* 8:263.

and debater, and from many accounts he was well aware of his talents. His affair with the young Heloise is well known, as is the violent retribution taken by his young lover's uncle. Perhaps Abelard's most controversial teaching regarded the atonement. Rather than understanding the death of Jesus as an atoning sacrifice for the sins of humanity, Abelard's exemplarist view of the atonement saw the cross as an image of love, as Jesus demonstrated for humanity the moral lesson of the suffering servant. The death of Jesus was a manifestation of God's love, not a sacrificial, atoning act. His unique view of the Trinity also became contentious when he defined the Father as Power, the Son as Wisdom, and the Holy Spirit as Goodness.[22]

For many modern readers, Abelard's doctrine may not seem as controversial as it must have appeared in the twelfth century. His attempt to combine philosophy and reason with theological introspection has been the method for critical thinkers since the renaissance. His insistence upon independent thinking was not accepted in the twelfth century in which he lived, as free enquiry was viewed as unfavorable to church discipline. However, one cannot assume that Abelard's doctrine alone caused so much concern for Bernard. One also cannot assume that Bernard desired the condemnation of Abelard because of the teacher's moral lapses, for in his condemnation of Abelard through a number of letters, Bernard does not mention Abelard's scandalous relationship with Heloise. Obviously, he was aware of the relationship. Either it was not the central issue of Bernard's problems with the scholar or else he believed it had nothing to do with the issue at hand. Clearly, this issue would have been an easy target for the Cistercian abbot. By not addressing this questionable behavior in Abelard's past, Bernard showed wise discretion. Evidence does exist, though, that before the events of 1139, Bernard and Abelard, other than being at odds professionally, felt no antagonism towards each other.[23]

The Abbot of Clairvaux was not opposed to scholasticism. The abbey itself had an extensive library, initiated by Bernard, which included the writings of many church Fathers and those of the Carolingian renaissance. For Bernard, the aspect of obtaining knowledge should always be grounded in love. One's study of theology should always lead one to union with God, having an effect on one's life. Seeking knowledge for its own sake, however, is an aspect of pride.[24] The use of reason for Bernard was a spiritual exercise

22. Peter Abelard, *Theologica Christiana*, 1.3.

23. Little, "Relations between St. Bernard and Abelard before 1139," 155–68.

24. *Hum* 13.41; *SBOp* 3:47.

that brings a person to humility. In his Sermons on the Song of Songs, Bernard teaches that any seeking of knowledge divorced from the goal of improving oneself or others is pride, vanity, and profiteering.

Another issue for Bernard in assessing an individual was determining one's motives. A person could be justified in a wrong decision if the individual had the proper objectives. The validity of one's intentions is a common theme for Bernard and may have been at the heart of his criticism of Abelard. Bernard writes that Abelard "is a man who does not know his limitations."[25] Abelard's intentions were selfish and ambitious, not the paradigm for a monk. This attitude amounted to a hypocritical presentation of himself and, subsequently, his ideas.

Bernard understood Abelard as one who sought knowledge for its own sake and for his own reputation. For the saintly abbot, this volatile combination needed to be quenched. In Bernard and Abelard were two opposing worlds: the old world of the church Fathers versus the emerging world of the scholastics. Had Abelard lived in a different age, his generation world have been more willing to accept his ideas. However, contending with the politically powerful Abbot of Clairvaux was his undoing, despite his scholastic popularity and personal pomp.

THE SECOND CRUSADE

When Bernard Paganelli, abbot of Saints Vincent and Anastasius and former monk of Clairvaux, was elected to the papacy as Eugenius III, the Cistercian arrival in the ecclesiastical world was ratified. Having a spiritual son as Pope gave Bernard considerable power, allowing him to influence the affairs of the world from a safe vantage behind the scenes, separated from public accountability. Bernard himself attests to this power in a letter to Eugenius, in which he relates the opinion of others who said, "it is not you but I who am the Pope."[26]

Bernard's health was declining and he was aging, yet he obeyed when asked by the new Pope engage in recruitment preaching throughout France for a crusade to free Edessa from Islamic occupation. To simplify political aspects, Eugenius desired a French crusade, and no one in the land was more capable than the esteemed Bernard to encourage the nobility and peasants to participate. Bernard was at the height of his reputation. Not

25. *Ep* 193; *SBOp* 8:44–45.
26. *Ep* 239; *SBOp* 8:120.

only had he resolved the papal schism a decade earlier, his former pupil now sat in Rome. In helping to resolve the schism, Bernard's intent was the preservation and reform of the church, for he saw in the person of Innocent II the means of keeping an evil presence out of the church.[27] Presented with the task of preaching a Crusade in France, Bernard once again saw an opportunity for ecclesiastical reform.

Bernard was known for his eloquent and persuasive preaching, and as he traversed France, Bernard's proclaimed words evoked images of a heavenly glory awaiting the crusaders in the Holy Land as they removed the Muslims from the holy places.[28] On 31 March 1146, below the hill town of Vézelay, Bernard preached to hundreds of people who came to see and be close to the holy monk. Following a moving message in support of the crusade, individuals began calling for crosses to stitch to their clothes to show their assent to make the journey to Jerusalem. Bernard himself offered his robe to be cut up and sewn into crosses for the masses. Even the proud and fashionable Eleanor of Aquitaine, Queen of France, seems to have been moved to action after hearing Bernard preach that day, and agreed to join her husband, King Louis VII, on the quest.

Encouraged by the hundreds of individuals who accepted his spiritual challenge to free the holy places from the heathen, Bernard wrote to Eugenius, "You ordered; I obeyed . . . I opened my mouth, I spoke; and at once the Crusaders have multiplied to infinity."[29] Bernard grew to believe that the spiritual importance of this crusade meant that more than just the French should be involved. Without consulting the Pope, he decided to take the message of the Crusade beyond the French borders and into Germany. Emperor Conrad had no intention of crusading with the young French King to Jerusalem, yet Bernard did not relinquish his attempts to stir Conrad to action. After several sermons in which the abbot failed to move the king, Bernard's eloquent preaching finally pierced the heart of Conrad two days after Christmas 1146 at Speier. Conrad pledged his support.

However, Pope Eugenius' plans for Conrad had nothing to do with his French crusade. Eugenius, facing difficulties with the Romans, was forced to leave Rome in 1145. He needed Conrad's help to suppress the Italians.

27. *Ep* 126; *SBOp* 7:309–19.

28. Although Bernard believed it was better to kill the Muslims than to let them kill holy Christians, his desire was their conversion to Christ. For a summary of the Cistercian view of the Crusades, see Kienzle, "Tending the Lord's Vineyard."

29. *Ep* 247; *SBOp* 8:141.

As he began to inquire about the state of the preparations of the crusade, he heard of Bernard's venture into Germany. Bernard, expanding the crusade beyond the sphere of the pope's desires, doused any help Conrad might have given Eugenius with the Italians. By sending an all-French crusading force, Eugenius wanted to avoid the divided command that led to the near defeat of the First Crusade.[30] Although he was asked simply to recruit for the effort, Bernard single-handedly changed the dynamic and politic of the crusade.

The crusade proved disastrous. The deplorable behavior of the German troops, the inept leadership of a young French king, the distrust between the two heads of state, and several distractions (including the presence of the French queen and her entourage), led to an embarrassing defeat at Damascus and the decimation of the European troops. Understandably, the blame was placed on Bernard.[31] People needed a scapegoat, and Bernard had recruited people with the promise of a heavenly rapture for everyone involved. Once the most powerful and influential figure in Europe, the tragic nature of the crusade resulted in Bernard losing much of his credibility, if not respect for his spirituality.

BERNARD'S SELF-UNDERSTANDING

Towards the end of his life, Bernard began to decline ecclesiastical invitations. In addition to frequent stomach ailments and physical frailties that plagued him for most of his life, he was growing weary of the many demands placed upon him, a situation he himself created that grew beyond his capacity to deal with it. In some ways, Bernard may have understood himself to be a caretaker of the entire church.[32] His love for the church, combined with his impulsive demeanor, resulted in his many activities away from his cloister at Clairvaux. Based on Bernard's understanding of the role and tasks of a monk, this existence was acceptable to him.[33] Because of his nature and understanding of love, he simply could not resist becoming involved in matters outside of Clairvaux.[34] In many ways, the

---

30. Runciman, *A History of the Crusades,* 2:257.

31. *Csi* 2.4; *SBOp* 3:413.

32. Fracheboud, "Je Suis La Chimèra De Mon Siècle," 132.

33. *Hum* 10.29; *SBOp* 3:39.

34. Sommerfeldt, *On the Spirituality of Relationship,* 113.

idea of Clairvaux as a remote haven for contemplation became a misnomer. Bernard's popularity was too strong a presence to keep people away.

In Bernard's later life, one can see some regret in his letters, as he questioned his own calling and even his very existence, as in the famous letter to a Carthusian prior in which he called himself a Chimæra and referred to his life as monstrous.[35] In writing to this Carthusian, who undoubtedly had many fewer involvements in the world than Bernard, the saint may have felt some embarrassment for not abandoning the world completely as his habit and tonsure indicated he had. Another instance of regret occurred during the papal schism, which kept the saint from joining the other Cistercian abbots in Chapter at Cîteaux around 1137. Bernard, ensnared in the political fallout of this scandal, realized his engagement with the church had become nothing but a burden to him. In the letter to his colleagues, he wrote that "life itself often becomes a burden to me."[36] The brutality of church politics was an aspect of ecclesiastical life had become a weight he could scarcely bear.

As one with a keen understanding of his own times and the people in it, Bernard could influence society with subtlety. After all, it was Bernard who was the focus of myth and hagiography and not Peter the Venerable, Suger, or other leaders. Bernard had no structural authority over anyone outside of his order, yet his influence permeated the whole of the European church. His personal sanctity and reforming vision moved many of those around him to respect him. They may not have liked him at times, but they nonetheless had deference towards him. As Jean Leclercq writes, Bernard never intended to be an eloquent diplomat of the church, renowned for his expertise in political or military matters. In his mind, he was a representative of Jesus Christ, crucified.[37] This vocational calling is all he knew to be, and in that regard, he became a polarizing figure in his own generation, even as Christ was in his.

35. *Ep* 250; *SBOp* 8:147.
36. *Ep* 145; *SBOp* 7:347.
37. Leclercq, *Bernard of Clairvaux and the Cistercian Spirit*, 70.

CHAPTER 2

Bernard and the Direction of Souls

THE MESSENGER OF GOD

Today, on the portico of the chateau atop Fontaines-les-Dijon—the site of Bernard of Clairvaux's childhood home—stands a nineteenth-century statue by Joseph Moreau. The sculpture depicts the saint holding a crucifix in his left hand. Curiously, the head of Christ is raised up and leaning towards Bernard's face, straining against the force of gravity. The eyes of the saint are focused squarely on the lifted face of the suffering Jesus. In his right hand, Bernard holds an opened scroll that he offers to the world, a message he has just received from the crucified Christ. This statue visually depicts the abbot's words in his eighty-second sermon on the Song of Songs, written near the end of his life, when he disclosed to his monks, "I have always shared with you without ill-will, and whatever I have been deemed worthy to receive I have poured out for you."

Bernard of Clairvaux had no doubt that his message for the church was from Christ himself and that his tireless interventions into the affairs of the world were labored as Christ's representative. This confidence, combined with a personal sanctity grounded in a healthy understanding of himself in relation to God, has allowed his influence to extend far beyond his own lifetime. To call Bernard simply a reformer does not represent his personal holiness. To call him merely a mystic does not characterize his worldly influence. Bernard of Clairvaux understood that his life was complex. He was a Cistercian monk removed from the world, yet his involvement in the world was anything but cloistered.

Bernard's letters, while providing an historical framework for his life and works, are also rich with the saint's reformation ideals through intentional spiritual direction. In fact, Bernard's agenda may be seen through the very structure of the saint's epistolary arrangement, a program based on the reform of the church. Bernard's letters contain an approach of spiritual direction based on a pragmatic method of human spirituality in which the objective of one's intimacy with God is not actualization of the self, but a manifestation of love for others. According to Bernard, loving oneself for the sake of God produces a love for the world as God loves the world. As he states in his letter to Prior Guy of the Grand Chartreuse, the law of God is a charity seeking not what is beneficial for the self but what is beneficial for others.[1]

Bernard's approach to loving God contained both affective and cognitive aspects. Human love for God requires both our heart and our mind working together through the guidance of the Holy Spirit. It is through these gifts of God that one can find God. While our minds help us navigate through the world, our hearts help navigate us to God. The use of both heart and mind is divinely granted. As beings created in the *imago Dei*, humans have the capacity for self-understanding. Thus, seeking one's true self is a prerequisite for seeking God. As Bernard writes in his first sermon for Advent, "Continuously run to your own self to meet your God." Self-examination as a discipline of Christian formation is a recurring theme in Bernard's letters. He exhorts everyone, from layperson to pope, to seek faithfulness to God through faithfulness to one's vocational call. This results in faithfulness to oneself.

A primary objective in Bernard's epistolary agenda was the restoration of the apostolic church through individual spiritual direction. This aim manifests itself in several recurring themes through the epistolary corpus. For Bernard, the reform of the church is possible only through the faithfulness and purity of heart of each person in the church, regardless of status, vocation, or gender. All persons have a responsibility for the church to be that which God has called it to be.

REGERE ANIMAS: THE DIRECTION OF SOULS

The term *regere animas*, as used in chapter 2 of Benedict's *Rule* when describing the qualifications of an abbot, refers to an abbot's responsibility in the spiritual care of the monks' souls (the literal translation is "directing souls"). Rather than an administrative or governing connotation, *regere* in

---

1. *Ep* 11.3; *SBOp* 7:54–55.

this instance infers that abbots should have a personal knowledge of their monks intimate enough to discern their relationship with Christ. An abbot's care of his monks' souls was not intended to be authoritative or controlling, but individualistic. Although Benedict diminishes the extent of the abbot's spiritual authority found in the *Regula Magistri*, he does maintain that the soul of each monk was the abbot's responsibility. The direction of souls is a ministry of guidance with people as they move toward the God-intended ideal for their lives. It begins with an inner examination of the self and results in the guidance of one or more individuals. This process requires willing submission on the part of the one being directed and practical discernment on the part of the one offering direction. The goal of each person in this relationship is a life in Christ so intimate that one's life becomes a living prayer. This living prayer enables one to discern the movement of the Holy Spirit in one's life. The direction of souls involves both explicit and implicit direction. *Explicit* direction manifests itself in rhetorical exhortation, as in a letter or sermon. *Implicit* direction is exhibited through the example of living a holy life. Rather than serving as a dictatorial spiritual parent, a director of souls is charged with maintaining a humble approach, knowing that he or she is merely the instrument of God in the individual's life. Traditionally, the direction of souls in the Christian tradition has included exhortation, prayer, community, and solitude.

Regere animas has been a part of the Christian tradition since the movement's inception. In fact, Christians have to look no further than to Jesus himself for its genesis. Through his sometimes challenging exhortations and his sanctity of life, Jesus of Nazareth became a messianic figure in first-century Palestine. Jesus referred to himself as a compassionate shepherd (John 10:11) and had compassion on the masses, whom he said were like sheep without a shepherd (Matt 9:36). The surviving letters of Paul, Peter, and other apostles are further examples of early spiritual direction, as they attempted to build both a doctrinal and organizational framework to the fledgling church. Both Jesus and the apostles expected their followers to heed their counsel. In addition to redemption, people needed someone to guide and care for them spiritually.

This approach to the spiritual growth of others continued from Jesus' teaching to the circulated writings of the apostle Paul and other early Christians. In the centuries that followed, both the ante- and post-Nicene Fathers provided a solid library of Christian teaching that encouraged believers to live faithfully to Christ. In this rapid ecclesiastical growth, spiritual direction in the Christian church was comprised of both personal and corporate elements. Personal spiritual direction included a superior and a supplicant and involved confession, penance, and restoration. The relationship between an abbot and a monk, or a priest and a congregant, are examples of personal spiritual direction. Corporate spiritual direction involves the transmission of spiritual counsel through the written or spoken word to more than one individual. This may manifest itself in a sermon, a letter, or a treatise.

The tradition of the early desert fathers as living in cenobitic houses of prayer influenced the later church with their focus on prayer as the center of their relationships with God and with each other. Existence on earth was not an end, but a means to heaven. By mutual accountability and prayer, their goal was to achieve Christ-likeness. These pre-Benedictine monks had no abbot, but a community who encouraged each other in prayer and contemplation, rather than in institutional sacramentalism. The desert fathers had no concept of church and state existing together. For them, the only Christian society was mystical—a community of prayer. The term used to describe the ones offering the spiritual direction became "fathers" and "mothers," in that they were fostering growth in the lives of their spiritual "children." One of the earliest extra-biblical references to this terminology was in Irenæus, who wrote that when any person is taught from the mouth of another, that person is the child of the person who offers the instruction; the latter is called the parent.[2]

Two primary streams of soul directing have existed in the history of the Christian church. The first is the monastic tradition, following a parent/child paradigm. In this tradition, the relationship between an abbot and a monk was paternal in nature, in which the monk is called to obey the abbot in all things, following the living example of the abbot. This model is most evident in the monastic tradition, particularly following Benedict's *Rule*. However, the *Rule* states that the abbot is the *pater monasterii*, not the *pater monachi*. The distinction is that while he is the father of the monastery, he is the *pastor*, or shepherd, of the monks. Scripturally, God is called both a shepherd and a father. The abbot, following the example of Christ, is given authority to administrate the affairs of the monastery. However, the abbot/shepherd does not own the flock of monks; rather, he is a steward of the flock for God.

2. *Against the Heresies*, 4.41.2.

For John Cassian (ca. 360–430), discretion is a key component in offering spiritual direction. The role of the master is to help the disciple discern and examine various thoughts or feelings in order to avoid pitfalls that would endanger the disciple's soul.[3] However, according to Cassian, not all persons had the spiritual qualities to serve as a master. A person who did not display the attributes of obedience and humility, and thus did not have a healthy grasp on discretion, was not worthy to mentor others.[4] Bernard echoed Cassian's view, as evidenced in several of his letters.[5]

Cassian asserted that true self-knowledge occurs through a life of humble transparency to one's elders, trusting their judgment as being the voice of God in one's life. Bernard certainly saw himself as having moral authority over others, and he was not apprehensive about sharing this. However, in early adulthood, Bernard's extreme ascetic lifestyle combined with the responsibility of establishing a new monastery caused his health to decline rapidly. When he would not listen to his monks when they expressed concern for their young abbot's health, they asked for help from the powerful and respected William of Champeaux, Bishop of Châlons-sur-Marne. Bernard had both respect for and obedience to William, and he accepted the bishop's order to move to a small hut behind the abbey church, relieved of all abbatial responsibilities.

The second stream of directing souls in the church is the priest/lay paradigm, in which a member of the secular clergy serves in a priestly role for laypersons in the administration of the sacraments, the teaching of doctrine, and the doing of good works. The distinction between priests and laity is made as early as Clement of Rome's "Letter to the Church at Corinth."[6] Tertullian, however, does not preclude the laity from possessing sacerdotal responsibilities, but reminds them that their sacramental privilege resides under the authority of the priests.[7] While abuses in this form spiritual direction tradition have plagued the church for centuries, attempts to provide for the spiritual well being of Christ's followers have been in existence since the composition of the Pastoral Epistles in the New Testament.

Confession, penance, and reconciliation have been seen historically as means to assurance and wholeness, as the priest represented the presence

3. Cassian, *Institutes,* 2.1.

4. Ibid., 2.3.

5. For example, see *Epp* 83, 193, 233, 346, 544.

6. In chapter 40 he says "the layperson is bound by the statutes of the layperson."

7. *On Baptism,* 17.

of Christ in the penitent individuals through the words of absolution. The sacramental nature of this process serves as a visible means for the penitent, through the priest, to be reconciled to God. In many ways, the priest who hears confession becomes a director of souls by helping people discern the presence of God in their lives. Traditionally, the ecclesiastical role of a priest, rather than the personal faithfulness of a priest, has given the priest the authority to bestow absolution. However, unless the priest is living a life of discipline and submission to God, the priest will not be able to offer sincere spiritual direction through the process of confession. As we shall see, Bernard of Clairvaux observed a clear correlation between the vocational and the personal.

The modern term "spiritual direction," although not found in patristic texts, is certainly present implicitly, particularly in light of the examples above from Benedict, Cassian, and Gregory. Although modern definitions of "spirituality" and "spiritual direction" have somewhat befuddled historical understandings of the terms, Benedict's use of the term *regere animas* contains ideas and themes analogous with historical usage of the term "spiritual direction." Bernard certainly would have understood Benedict's use of the term *regere animas*, and the definitions he offers in his writings are in harmony with chapter 2 of the *Rule*. Therefore, despite the rhetorical limitations of cultural transference, the terms *regere animas*, "direction of souls," "spiritual counsel," and "spiritual direction" are used interchangeably in this work.

REGERE ANIMAS AND BERNARD OF CLAIRVAUX

Bernard of Clairvaux's understanding of this process was clearly in the parent/child model of directing souls, as evidenced throughout the epistolary corpus. In a majority of his letters, the abbot plays the part of the wise father offering counsel to his son.[8] In a few letters to popes, Bernard even assumes the role of the pope's spiritual father.[9] Even Bernard's letters to laity follow this model of spiritual direction, as the abbot writes as the authoritative voice of God the Father to his children.[10] Curiously missing from the corpus are substantial examples of Bernard humbling himself before his own ecclesiastical authorities! As a Cistercian, Bernard's strict reliance upon

8. *Epp* 1, 8, 22, 25, 69, 72, 83, 161, 230, 313, 321, 360, 254, 143, 142, 34.

9. *Epp* 161, 180, 235, 309, 273.

10. *Epp* 104, 112, 116, 242, 255, 421, 457, 496, 515.

the Benedict's *Rule* would have influenced his understanding and con-textualization of *regere animas*. At its core, the *Rule* serves as a document of spiritual direction. It describes the ideal Christian community and the means for spiritual growth through community and liturgical prayer, and demonstrated through submission, work, and humility.

Bernard of Clairvaux uses the phrase *regere animas* twice in his works, both in the *Sermons on the Song of Songs*. The first usage is in Sermon 10, in which he refers to virtues necessary in the lives of those who have under-taken the task of directing souls. He compares directors of souls to mothers whose breasts are full for the taking, although some, who have no maternal instincts, are concerned only for their own well-being and not for the souls of those they endeavor to nurture. The task of caring for another's soul is a selfless enterprise, requiring personal sacrifice with no agenda other than Christ sustaining the individual being guided.

The second usage of *regere animas* in Bernard is found in Sermon 58. In describing the nature of *regere animas*, he writes, "The soul who is more complete is invited to correct others, to instruct them, to save them, as long as he is assigned this ministry not by his own ambition, but by the call of God, as Aaron was." This insightful passage involves the methods for achieving *regere animas*, as well as the personal qualifications of the person who desires to undertake it. By stating Aaron, Bernard sets a priestly stan-dard on the one offering the soul-guidance. These two examples from Ber-nard are squarely in the same understanding of *regere animas* mentioned in Benedict.

Bernard of Clairvaux's understanding of spiritual direction would have come from the teachings of Jesus and the epistles, as well as the church Fathers, upon whom many medieval ecclesiastical leaders placed a strong reliance. Although Bernard's use of Scripture was expansive, his use of explicit quotations from extra-biblical Christian writers was limited. However, this is not to imply that Bernard did not reveal his patriarchal sources. For example, similarities exist between his understanding of hu-man freedom and Augustine's discussion of the subject in *De libero arbitrio*, although, where the Bishop of Hippo places the *imago Dei* in the human intellect, the abbot of Clairvaux perceives it primarily as being realized in the human will.[11]

Bernard's implicit reliance upon John Cassian came from Benedict's predisposition towards Cassian: the stress Cassian placed on the importance

11. Anderson, "Bernard of Clairvaux," 99.

of both *actio* and *contemplatio* certainly held importance to Benedict, and subsequently to the Cistercians. Cassian's approach to spiritual mentoring appealed to Benedict, who incorporated these terms into his Rule. Submission to an elder in Cassian is a primary means of spiritual growth.[12] In fact, Cassian writes that a monk who does not heed the spiritual counsel of his elders has allowed the devil to lead away his soul to death.[13]

To understand Bernard's concept of spiritual direction, one must acknowledge the abbot's reliance upon Pope Gregory I (540–604). Bernard drew from Gregory a clear sense of the roles of oversight of the ordained ministry, including a methodology for the care of souls.[14] Bernard had a strong connection with this pontiff who relied heavily upon monastic leaders to achieve his sweeping sixth-century reforms. Bernard cites Gregory ten times in his Letters, referring primarily to the pope's *Pastoral Rule*. The breadth of styles exhibited in Bernard's letters demonstrates Bernard's inclination to heed Gregory's counsel regarding the care of others. In his *Pastoral Rule*, Gregory refers to the directing of souls as the art of all arts. No skill is as valuable as guiding someone's soul to God. To be a "physician of the heart" (*medici carnis*) requires spiritual depth and discernment, and is a responsibility not be taken lightly. The spiritual care of others requires spiritual discernment so the shepherd can best understand the most proper means of communicating with someone. Likewise, Bernard, emulating the example of his predecessor, took care (regarding both content and style) when composing letters to people in different societal strata and in diverse ecclesiastical situations.

Bernard believed that all people in a monastery, not merely priors and abbots, had the capacity to offer *regere animas* because they were part of a spiritual covenant.[15] Their activity in the monastic community and their life of prayer bound them together in spiritual intimacy. This combination of action and contemplation produces a unique bond in the monastic community in which each person has a responsibility to the other. Despite the hierarchical nature of monasticism, monks and abbots exist for each other in a spiritual kinship. For example, through an abbot's pastoral care for a monk, he himself may experience inner transformation through his offering of charity and counsel. As a model of Christian community, a

12. *Institutes*, 4.7.

13. *Conferences*, 2.11.

14. Evans, *Bernard of Clairvaux*, 159.

15. Smith, "Contemplation and Action," 18.

monastery was the ideal place for individuals to encounter Christ—sometimes through daily encounters with others who have a shared commitment to the Christian charism.

WAS BERNARD A DIRECTOR OF SOULS?

As an abbot who was frequently absent from his spiritual sons at Clairvaux, did Bernard have the capacity to offer them spiritual direction? With the rapid growth of the monastery compared with their abbot's travel schedule, it hardly seems possible that Bernard was able to know his spiritual sons very well. More likely than not, the priors and Clairvaux must have assumed much of the spiritual guidance as their abbot's representative. One must empathize with young men who left their families at the emotive preaching of Bernard to find that the person they believed would guide them through the spiritual life spent much of his time in other places. However, Bernard strongly believed that his role was to offer spiritual direction not only to his own monks at Clairvaux, but to the entire church, as well.

If the direction of souls involves a spiritual parent and the spiritual child, Bernard had no misgivings about assuming the role of the father, even when writing to the pope. However, much of the spiritual counsel Bernard offers is not through face-to-face encounters, but through epistolary rhetoric. The growth of this medium expanded rapidly in the early twelfth century, and Bernard was not hesitant to utilize it. The spread of Bernard's influence in society is testament that through his writings, he was having a dramatic effect on the church. The measure of spiritual directional success cannot be measured quantitatively, however. Since Bernard (reluctantly or not) placed the spiritual state of the church on his own shoulders, the success of his spiritual influence should be measured against the climate of the church. Certainly, Cistercian growth flowered during his lifetime, culminating in the ascension of a Cistercian pope near the end of Bernard's life. His preaching stirred thousands of people to action, and his counsel to Kings and other notables altered the course of history. His efforts were tireless, and what has remained of his writings have influenced Christians for more than eight hundred years. If Bernard saw himself as a spiritual director, he would understand his role as a spiritual father to the church through his interactions with individuals within the church.

In a broad sense, each of Bernard's writings can be considered examples of spiritual direction. He wrote his sermons, treatises, and his sentences to encourage others in their relationship with Christ. His sarcastically written *Apologia* against the excesses of Cluny was Bernard's attempt to demonstrate that the Cistercian way was the preferred means to union with Christ. Through his writings, Bernard confidently placed himself in the position of a spiritual elder and advisor to the world. Michael Casey has observed that Bernard's spiritual influence can be understood as a series of ever-widening circles. He first imparted values to his family, then to Clairvaux, then to the monastic world, then to the affairs of the church, and finally to all of Europe.[16] In each of these spheres of influence, Bernard attempted to persuade those around him to seek the divine in all areas of individual and societal life. His writings were his attempt to broaden this message that he believed was given to him by God.

However, since the present definition of *regere animas* involves the willing submission on the part of the one being directed, the issue of Bernard as a director of souls becomes complicated. The influence of Bernard as a spiritual director via the medium of letter writing is difficult to discern. Examining the actions of individuals following the reception of one or more of Bernard's letters may indicate an influence from the abbot of Clairvaux, but their actions could have resulted from many factors, not just Bernard's counsel. Yet, his influence on the church and European society in his day is generally accepted. Unquestioned is his imprint on the lives of individuals following his death. Since spirituality involves dynamics of the heart, the use of quantitative analysis as a means of measuring spiritual growth is problematic. Bernard believed he was a director of souls in the tradition of the church Fathers and Benedict's *Rule*. Because Bernard's life and teachings had such influence upon individuals and the society in which he lived, the assumption of this book is that Bernard was indeed a spiritual director to some, but not to everyone, with whom he communicated.

REGERE ANIMAS IN BERNARD'S LETTERS

Bernard did not simply compose and compile his corpus of letters at random. Like most everything else he did, the saint had an agenda. He knew his letters would be read by many people, influencing more than just the persons to whom they were addressed. By looking at both the letter recipients and the general content, scholars can discern basic objectives that Bernard could have had in mind when composing his many epistles.

16. Casey, *Athirst for God*, 2.

Nearly every letter Bernard wrote contained some element of spiritual direction. In fact, some of Bernard's greatest wisdom is found in the pages of his letters. Through this correspondence, we see Bernard in the real world, dealing with real issues facing both individuals and the church. Sometimes Bernard's counsel was emotive, as in his impassioned letter to a nun who had left her profession[17] and his letter to the Roman people when they rebelled against the pope.[18] In other situations, Bernard offers counsel disguised as guilt.[19] Whatever the advice, Bernard felt that he had the authority and wisdom to offer it, even to the pope. Once the modern reader is able to sift through the formalities of twelfth-century letter-writing protocol, Bernard emerges as a transparent leader, seldom hiding his emotions, his beliefs, or his agendas. Perhaps his willingness to expose his heart and soul through his letters makes them so interesting to read. While we do not know the effect all of his letters had on the recipients nor the decisions they made, it is easy to imagine more than one individual rolling his or her eyes and taking a deep breath before unsealing one of Bernard's epistles.

Although the spiritual counsel offered in the body of his letters was plentiful, the introductions to his epistles, are quite interesting, as well—sometimes setting the tone for the letter that followed. For example, in a letter written to Louis *"le gros"* ("the fat") King of France regarding the Council of Pisa in 1134, Bernard writes, "To the most excellent Louis, King of France . . . Bernard, styled abbot of Clairvaux sends health from the King of Kings and Lord of Lords."[20] In this seemingly simple introduction, Bernard presents the king with two subtle reminders. The first is that Louis is not the ultimate authority in France. He is subordinate to Almighty God. The second is that Bernard was speaking on God's behalf, so Louis had better pay attention to the letter that follows. Rather than serving as a simple manipulative power play, Bernard is able to give the king counsel without explicitly offering Louis unwanted advice. Louis should remember his place as a child of God, and not as an unaccountable supreme ruler.[21]

---

17. *Ep* 114; *SBOp* 7:291–93.

18. *Ep* 243; *SBOp* 8:130–34.

19. *Ep* 197; *SBOp* 8:53.

20. *Ep* 255; *SBOp* 8:161.

21. A similar introduction is found in *Letter 92* to Henry I, King of England, in which Bernard hopes that "in his earthly kingdom he may faithfully serve and humbly obey the King of Heaven." *SBOp* 7:241.

As a man who had fled the world by becoming a Cistercian monk, Bernard should have been an outsider to most of the Christian world, making his ever-present advice giving even more curious. His only title other than priest was abbot, and he turned down the archbishopric of Rheims in 1139. Perhaps his reasoning in refusing to accept the appointment was that he did not want the accountability that came with the role. That he frequently encouraged individuals in his letters to be obedient to God by accepting new positions offered to them is peculiar when one examines his own refusal to become a bishop. On the other hand, he may have possessed such a strong vocational call that he knew more than the pope or anyone else where God wanted him to be. In a letter to the King of France, Bernard responds to his potential election as the Archbishop of Rheims by stating that he cannot accept the position, for, in a play on words, "no one is better known to me than myself; no one knows me as well as I know myself."[22] For Bernard, self-knowledge is vital to understanding one's vocation.

While Bernard believed that the real city of God, Jerusalem, is the only place where individuals can find Christ,[23] he understood Clairvaux as the world's New Jerusalem: a refuge from and hope of the world, and the most promising place for individuals to be conformed to Christ's image.[24] Through this New Jerusalem, God would provide the means for individuals to find unity in God through an escape from the world. He exhorts individuals to flock to the *city of refuge*.[25] For the monk, this flight from the world can occur anywhere, however, and not just at Clairvaux or within the Cistercian order. He believed that the monastery shared Jerusalem's distinction, conferring upon its residents the spiritual benefits of the places made holy by Christ in his daily activities in the physical Jerusalem.[26]

Bernard was not alone in his understanding that the safety of the cloister was the most expeditious way to God, but he was distinctive in his belief that Christians could find unity with God, including the laity. Bernard's anthropology allowed individuals the freedom of introspection. By placing the importance of the human being in the eyes of God as a central theme in his writings, Bernard offered an approach to the direction of souls that extended the capacity for intimacy with God to those on the outside of the

---

22. *Ep* 449; *SBOp* 8:426.

23. *SC* 76.257; *SBOp* 1:259.

24. *Ep* 64; *SBOp* 7:157.

25. *Conv* XX.1.37; *SBOp* 4:113.

26. Leclercq, *The Love of Learning*, 55.

monastic walls. Bernard's desire for all persons was not necessarily a conversion to monastic life (although that was the ideal), but rather a conversion to God.[27] Bernard's foremost concern for all people, regardless of their state or status in life, was quite straightforward: how can a sinner return to God and be united with God?[28] Bernard believed this is best achieved separated from the world where one can seek God without distraction, but he understood that not all persons were called to the monastic vocation. For Bernard, the church is the spouse of Christ arrayed with many jeweled adornments of religious orders.[29] He likened the church to Joseph's multicolored robe, in which the seamless robe has colors representing the varied peoples within the church: married couples, celibates, monks, canons regular, cenobites, and hermits.[30]

RECURRING THEMES

Through careful examination of Bernard's letters, we can discern several distinct, recurring themes throughout the epistolary corpus that transcend recipient categorization. Based on the context of the letters, these themes form a synthesis of the abbot's reformational and restorational agendas. First, Bernard held that individuals must be re-formed into Christ's image through humility, obedience, and self-understanding. This personal reformation leads one to Christ through prayer, and enables one to exist as a living prayer. Second, he believed that the church, rather than reformation, needed a restoration to its former state in the days of the apostles and Fathers of the church. Its priorities and methodology had become far removed from the simple faith of church leaders in the days of old. Bernard believed this was attainable only through prayer and meditation, primarily through the monastic movements in the church. Third, society could achieve Christ's agenda on earth only through the union of church and state. Finally, Bernard stressed the woven bond between the ecclesiastical and the personal. Through the obedience of each person in the church, the church would once again return to its apostolic glory as the faithful Bride of Christ.

27. Renna, "The City in Early Cistercian Thought," 5–19.
28. Kereszty, "Relationship between Anthropology and Christology," 271–99.
29. Pennington, "Straight from the Shoulder," 189–98.
30. *Apo* 6; *SBOp* 3:86.

These themes weave together to form a thematic synthesis: the importance of self-understanding as a means to intimacy with Christ. These five basic themes are united by this over-arching idea in Bernard's letters. According to Bernard in his epistles, one cannot live faithfully to Christ without first having a healthy understanding of oneself, one's vocation, and one's surroundings. For the married couple, Bernard writes that they must have a complete understanding of how being married relates to their relationship with Christ. For the monk, this self-awareness is grounded in humility and obedience. For the pope and other ecclesiastical leaders, without self-knowledge they will damage not only their own souls, but also the souls of those under them. Bernard desired that the church be restored to the priorities of the days of the apostles. He believed that the inner reformation of the persons who comprise the Body of Christ would enable this to happen through the workings of the Holy Spirit, which results in the transformation of the culture into the faithful Body of Christ.

CHAPTER 3

An Introduction to the Letters of Bernard

CHRISTIAN EPISTOLARY RHETORIC BEGAN with the apostle Paul, who left the church several examples of the use and structure of letters. The liturgical use and canonization of his letters clearly demonstrates the medium of epistolary correspondence had importance and authority for the early Christians. The importance of letters grew with the church, particularly following the Council of Carthage in 397, and as Christian influence expanded geographically. The function of ecclesial letter writing, particularly in the early medieval period, became more of a means for communication than for the explication of doctrine. By the twelfth century, letters had become an indispensable aspect of society, serving in various capacities from personal correspondence to papal bulls. Clearly, the use of letters became a central tool for the reformation agenda of Bernard of Clairvaux.

NATURE AND PURPOSE OF EPISTOLARY RHETORIC IN TWELFTH-CENTURY EUROPE

As governments, courts, and businesses expanded economically, the need for effective, clear communication became vitally important. Epistolary rhetoric, rather than classical oratory, became essential in the expanding society. Due to the complexity of much of the legal language in written communication, rulers found the need for educated professionals in the epistolary arts who were trained in classic Ciceronian rhetoric.[1] These letter writers had the task of composing letters that were not necessarily literary in nature, but administrative, an undertaking that must have

1. Kristeller "Humanism and Scholasticism," 346–74.

seemed tedious at times. Most of these secular letters had no date ascribed to them, an aspect that according to Giles Constable is more of interest to modern scholars than it was to medievals.[2] Perhaps the view was that royal pronouncements transcended time, so no dates were needed. English and French royal decrees taking an epistolary form were commonplace, making these letters official public documents. The reason for this use of letters may have been the simplicity of using a common form for general communications and decrees.

Because the ability to write was rare among the laity, including the royalty, having trust in one's scribe was of utmost importance. The king would not sign a letter, but rather fix his seal to the letter. It is easy to imagine why the king's "chancellor," the one entrusted with the keeping of the king's seals, was such a prestigious position. Our twenty-first-century worldview makes the illiterateness of the royalty seem unimaginable. However, the communal aspect of medieval society made this reliance acceptable. A chancellor who enjoyed the power and life security of his position desired that his written communication portray the king in the highest possible manner.

Not everyone viewed the rising prominence of written correspondence favorably. Latin poets of the time, including Bernard Silvestris, Alan of Lille, and Peter of Blois, were well aware of the function and importance of letter writing, yet the restrictions placed on the rhetorical creativity of such letters seemed to stifle their creative minds. They already faced opposition from the church for their writings, some of it ribald, but among the secular nobility, the writings of these artisans of rhetoric enjoyed general popularity.

The influx of letter writing in the Western church began with the papal letter, which functioned as the instrument for daily business. Letters sent from Rome to the corners of the church established papal authority in places the pope would never visit. As the European civilization and economy expanded, so did the number of papal letters. Richard Southern has shown the number of surviving papal letters from the first half of the tenth century under Silvester II (999–1003) to the papacy of John XXII (1316–24) expanded from ten per year under Silvester to just over 3,600 per year under John.[3]

---

2. Constable, *Letters and Letter-Collections*, 23.

3. Southern, *Western Society and the Church*, 108–9.

As a papal letter could serve as a granter of power and privilege, abbots of powerful monasteries often sought such letters for papal benefits. The tithe exemption granted to the Clairvaux by Innocent II as a reward for Bernard's tireless efforts during the papal schism is just one example of a papal benefit given through the means of a letter. Popes could best publicize their generosity through tangible letters that would be read aloud and cherished by the recipients. As the recognized leader of the church, the pope could use his letters to demonstrate the acceptable use of epistles in the operation of church business. While popes used letters for their own business and the promotion of their own agendas, they found others with opinions divergent from theirs could do the same, precipitating the need for papal documents regarding official church doctrines and governmental controls.[4] Likewise, a bishop used letters to exert control over his diocese, including the reception of tithes and the execution of administrative business.

Not only did twelfth-century ecclesiastic leaders follow the example of the secular uses of the letter, they also provided leadership to the genre by establishing schools for the education of the letter writers. That the church, particularly the monastic community, would educate would-be epistolary scribes is not surprising. Although the *Rule* of Benedict does not explicitly prescribe an educational program for the monks, it does promote a grammatical culture.[5] In the thirteenth century, these schools, particularly in Italy and France, began to focus more on the form of the letter than the content in the letter.

Some have suggested the religious renewal movements of the late eleventh and twelfth centuries were due, in part, to letters used for the enlistment of prelates for the monasteries and students for the universities.[6] Bernard certainly used letters in his recruitment of young noblemen. In the instance an individual, moved to action by the saint's emotional and authoritative preaching, had promised himself to Clairvaux, the saint would send the person letters until the future prelate surrendered his secular life for the cloister.

For monasteries, a monastic "postal service" allowed isolated monasteries to communicate with each other and hear news from the outside world. This means of interconnectedness was not a contradiction to Benedict, for chapter 54 of the *Rule* states monks may receive letters only

4. Morris, "Medieval Media," 14.

5. Irvine, *The Making of Textual Culture,* 189–95.

6. Constable, *Letters,* 32.

through the abbot, making them communal documents. Letters also assisted monks in the vow of stability, as they afforded the monastic community information about the outside world without ever having to leave their monastery. Due to the expense and great effort in composing and sending letters, monastic letters were received with great joy and solemnity, and many became part of the abbey's library.[7] Word that a monk had received a letter soon reached everyone in the abbey, and everyone would want to hear what the letter had to say. Letters brought such joy to the sequestered brothers because letters reminded them they were not a solitary community but part of a greater association of faith.

Letter-writers like Bernard understood their correspondence would more than likely be read to the greater monastic community, so they took great pains to ensure the language and tone of the letter was not only engaging, but at times filled with grandiose language. While these letters followed the basic medieval model of salutation, introduction, narrative, petition, and conclusion, Cistercian letters, unlike their Benedictine counterparts, did not always adhere to the stricter letter writing art forms, opting instead to model simplicity of form and content. Nevertheless, both Cistercian and Benedictine letter writers took the opportunity to address the spiritual needs of those in the monastic community, and would often include in their letters exhortations and homilies about perseverance in the monastic life, obedience to their abbot, and the virtues of their calling.[8]

In addition to letters written for a specific purpose of either business or spiritual counsel, many letters in the twelfth century were written merely for personal reasons. These letters of friendship were common among both laity and monks and serve as examples of the importance of spiritual friendships in the period.[9] At times, these letters contain nothing more than expressions of love or requests for prayer. If the sender and the recipient have a close enough relationship, the letter may even have no purpose other than serving as a friendly, humorous note.[10] Personal letters were never securely personal, but they extended one's understanding of community and belonging and made an expanding Europe seem not so large.

---

7. Leclercq provides a very descriptive narrative of the entire letter-writing process, from the initial parchment creation to the final letter reception ritual in *The Love of Learning and the Desire for God*, 176–79.

8. Leclercq, "Lettres de vocation à la vie monastique," 169–97.

9. Leclercq, *Love of Learning*, 180–81.

10. One example is Bernard's *Ep* 402; *SBOp* 8:382.

For women, particularly in the nobility and monastic communities, letter writing could have liberating effects. Marginalized socially and politically, medieval women found freedom in the ability to share their opinions through written letters. The written word conveyed a sense of authority in the one who sent it. For most women, even those in the courts of state, letter writing was the only authority they would experience. Through letters, women could transcend social and educational barriers, giving women a voice in society. Evidence of letters written to women in Europe exists as early as the reign of Charlemagne, when Alcuin wrote to Gisela, the king's sister, asking for her opinions on his commentary on the Gospel of John.[11] The exchange of letters between Hildegard of Bingen and Bernard of Clairvaux serves as another example of letters written across the boundaries of gender. Perhaps the most famous medieval letters written between a man and a woman, the letters of Abelard and Heloise, have been questioned as fraudulent; however, the importance of these letters lies in their intimacy. The lovers could not assume that these letters would have been kept out of public examination, particularly considering Abelard's scandalous career and personal issues.

Although personal correspondence was not always personal, these letters served a significant role in the anthropological development of the twelfth century through the standardized communication of ideas. As society gained an appreciation of the importance of the self and attempted to find a healthy anthropological balance in that recognition, personal correspondence allowed individuals to express their emotions and ideas to others. This freedom was always tempered with the social accountability of knowing others would have access to the letter.

THE *ARS DICTAMINIS*

The increasing use of letter writing in medieval Europe ushered in a new rhetorical genre, based primarily on the epistolographic teachings and methods of Cicero.[12] As much of the European world was becoming increasingly bureaucratic and institutionalized, written communication found structure and procedure. Schools specifically developed to teach the art of letter writing emerged throughout Europe, producing manuals called

11. Classen, "Female Epostolary Literature" 3–13.
12. Constable, "Letters and Letter Collections," 20–21.

ars dictaminis or, in a general sense, *dictamen*.[13] Demand for individuals skilled in epistolary rhetoric began to rise in the early twelfth century, and these professionals could make a good living.

Bernard's inconsistent use of the *ars dictaminis* reflects his insistence on the importance of the message of the letter over the style with which the letter is recorded. Still, as an educated man of the church, he was aware of the art. His obvious and intentional deviation from the appropriate style added drama to his letters in order to illicit the greatest response possible from the recipient(s). In certain instances, when he did exceed the limitations of the *modus epistolaris*, he acknowledged this error, as in *On the Steps of Humility and Pride*, in which he apologizes for exceeding the approved epistolary limits, and that the recipient could call the epistle either a book or a letter as he sees fit.[14] It mattered little to Bernard what style he used or how individuals would define the genre of his writings.

AN INTENTIONAL ARRANGEMENT?

In the initial edition of Bernard's letters, compiled between 1126 and 1145 (known as the *Brevis*), the letters are arranged in the following order: 65, 78, 254, 11, 12, 1, 107, 117, 69, etc.[15] However, by the time of the larger collection of letters, assembled shortly before his death (known as the *Longior* collection), the order of the letters changed dramatically, taking a different arrangement, beginning with letters 1–44, 311, 45–82, and so on.[16] As Leclercq demonstrates, these letters are as edited and polished as any of Bernard's other works, signifying the saint's intention for them to be published. The restructuring of the letters demonstrates even further that Bernard was interested not only in the content of the individual letters, but also in the theological and spiritual significance of the corpus as a whole (including their arrangement).[17] One must remember that the nature and function of medieval letters were much more than merely disseminating information and expressing greetings. They had the power of affecting

---

13. Murphy, *Rhetoric in the Middle Ages*, 202.

14. *Prae* 61; *SBOp* 3:294.

15. The complete list is cited by Leclercq in "Lettres de S. Bernard: Histoire ou Littérature?," 21.

16. Ibid., 22.

17. Smerillo, "*Caritas* in the Initial Letters of St. Bernard," 118–36.

public events, and at times served as prominent aspects of public activity and thought.

The order of the letters by Bernard and his editor Geoffrey offers an outline of the duties and responsibilities to those in various positions in the church.[18] This synthesizes with Bernard's lifelong desire for general reform in the church, and may provide at least one reason why the letter to Robert is at the forefront of the corpus.[19] Leclercq suggests that the order of Bernard's letters is both chronological and doctrinal in nature, offering an editorial on the monastic life. Perhaps Bernard's intent was to provide through his letters a sort of reflection of the early twelfth-century church, commenting that for both historical events and individuals, reform could only take place through the interior, personal reform of each person in their various roles in the church at large.

Two primary letter arrangements exist today. In the *Sancti Bernardi Opera*, Leclercq and Rochais follow Mabillon's order for the sake of simplicity and historical consistency, and to follow Bernard's supposed doctrinal and reformist arrangement. James, on the other hand, in his English translation of the letters from Mabillon, places the letters in a rough chronological order that follows either events or groups of the same recipients.

Had the James edition been the standard corpus for hundreds of years, his semi-chronological numbering and order would be preferred to Mabillon/Leclercq. James groups Bernard's letters chronologically by both event and recipient (including groups of letters to abbots, women, runaway monks, etc.), so searching the corpus for a specific letter is more convenient than in Leclercq. The Leclercq edition follows the *Longior* arrangement from Geoffrey and Bernard. While this arrangement might be enlightening for antiquity's sake, the more modern James order allows both scholars and popular readers to engage Bernard more easily than Leclercq, and to have a greater comprehension of the actual events and people to whom Bernard wrote.[20] Truly, both Leclercq and James have scholastic importance, the former more as a historical and critical study and the latter as a spiritual exercise and easy reference. A complete understanding of the saint's letters,

18. Leclercq, "Recherches sur la collection des épîtres de Saint Bernard," 205–19.

19. This letter to Robert is the supposed "miracle letter," which he dictated in the rain. As the scribe wrote the letter, the parchment miraculously stayed dry. According to the *Vita Prima*, this is the reason why this letter to Robert was placed at the forefront of the letter collection.

20. For example, James's *Epp* 236–49 correspond to *Epp* 187–94, 327, and 330–38 in Leclercq's numbering system.

however, can only be appreciated with a comprehension of both editions, for the sake of both for content and arrangement. However, since all editions of Bernard's letters except for James follow the Mabillon/Leclercq edition, it must be seen as the preferred edition for scholars.

BERNARD'S EPISTOLARY RECIPIENTS

Bernard's letter-writing activity encompassed most of European society. Other than peasants, who for the most part could not read, and members of the lower-class laity, who generally had little involvement in the affairs of the church or government, Bernard wrote extensively to a wide range of people groups. His letters seemed to be addressed to two specific, yet broad categories of individuals. The first group was those who were in positions of influence. This included members of the secular nobility, those in ecclesiastical offices in Rome and elsewhere, and abbots. The second group of people who received letters from the saint was individuals who had an interest in either a more disciplined spiritual life or a monastic vocation. This could be anyone, including members of the nobility or common laypeople. In some cases, the recipients in this group were those who had strayed from their spiritual vocation and thus received a stern, sometimes gracious, scolding from the abbot.

Although these two categories of recipients are clear in the corpus of Bernard's letters, the breakdown of recipients is far more complex. For example, recipient categories sometimes overlapped each other, since nearly every one of the saint's letters had some form of spiritual counsel. Bernard frequently combined political church reform issues with personal spiritual counsel in a single letter. In the Leclercq edition, 360 letters are addressed to ecclesiastical recipients. The remaining 103 letters are to lay people. For a medieval monk, Bernard wrote a surprisingly large number of letters to women compared to the number of letters to women by his contemporaries.[21] With regard to letters to ecclesiastical recipients, the two most common recipients were popes (96) and abbots (94). In the lay arena, Bernard wrote most commonly to simple laypersons (27) and kings (21). Geographically, the breadth of Bernard's recipients spanned all of Roman Catholic Europe and into the Kingdom of Jerusalem.

Bernard wrote fewer than thirty-five letters to monks. Considering the large collection of authentic letters in existence, this small number seems

21. Leclercq, *Women and St. Bernard of Clairvaux*, 33.

surprising. A monk himself, one would think that Bernard would have more to say to his brothers. However, as one who desired to see the church reformed, Bernard understood that the reforming would come from those within the political system of the church; hence, his furious letter writing to popes, bishops, and abbots. Another reason for the limited number of letters to monks is that Bernard did not want to interfere in the relationships between monks and their abbots, so his letters to monks are usually designed to build or re-build the bond between spiritual fathers and sons.

Bernard wrote nearly one-hundred letters to abbots. Although Bernard could not have been a particularly good abbot, he nevertheless had much advice to offer his abbatial colleagues.[22] A slight contrast exists in these letters between letters to Cistercian abbots and letters to non-Cistercian abbots. Bernard wrote to his Cistercian abbots with a familial style, though this could mean a scathing rebuke. To abbots outside of his order, Bernard's style is more formal than that in letters written to Cistercian abbots. He congratulated non-Cistercian abbots for reforms they had taken or for how they had dealt with persecutions because of their reforms.

In his letters to members of the ecclesiastical hierarchy, Bernard was quite bold. Bernard's letters to bishops and popes are perhaps the most enjoyable to read, for it is in these letters that we see Bernard at his literary finest. At times, his emotion and spontaneity spring forth from the letters as if they were written hastily and then whisked away. That Bernard included them in the *Longior* collection of his letters demonstrates that he was not regretful for writing them (although we do not know the extent to which they were edited).

For the most part, Bernard's letters to bishops are less forward than his letters to popes. He always showed respect to these church leaders, even when he did not agree with decisions they made or the way they managed their personal lives. Bernard's letters to bishops cover many topics. Many of these serve as Bernard's reply to their own correspondence to him. At times Bernard offers both practical and spiritual advice to bishops, hinting that he knows more about how they should conduct their business than they do.[23] Yet, Bernard did not exclude those in the bishopric from an emotional appeal every now and then. For example, to the bishops of Aquitaine Bernard wrote a long, scathing letter against Gerard of Angoulême, who supported the antipope Anacletus II. One can imagine Bernard dictating this letter of

22. Leclercq, *Bernard of Clairvaux and the Cistercian Spirit*, 37.

23. E.g., *Epp* 25–29; *SBOp* 7:78–84.

action while pacing in his cell. It begins with a charge: "Courage is gained in peace, proved in adversity, and confirmed in victory. The time has come, most reverent and holy fathers, for you to take courage, if you have any, and bestir yourselves to action."[24] With opening lines like this, the bishops had better pay attention to what followed.

Since Bernard had a hand in the editing and arrangement of so many of his letters, one may wonder why either Bernard (or particularly Geoffrey) did not redact many of these strong, emotional letters to ecclesiastical authorities. Certainly, these letters portray the saint as an emotional leader and an intruder into the affairs of others—not a popular way to secure one's own canonization! While not all of the papal letters were included in the *Longior* edition, several letters were included, and not all of them portrayed Bernard in a seemingly positive way. Speculation is an overly simplistic way to make judgments, but in some cases that is all that scholars can do. Following Leclercq's hypothesis that the overarching desire of Bernard and Geoffrey regarding the letters was the reform of the church, one can conclude that these papal and bishopric letters, through their strong language, portrayed Bernard as a reformer of the church who was not afraid to confront the leaders of his day. They are also a statement that the abbot had the respect of the ecclesiastical authorities, who were able to stomach such epistolary language.

Bernard wrote more than seventy-five letters to members of the nobility, including nearly thirty letters to kings and emperors. The content of these letters varies, but most include Bernard's political views on a number of issues, and many include spiritual counsel or warnings of some sort. No less than twenty letters are addressed to Counts or Countesses, several of whom were Cistercian benefactors.

These letters demonstrate Bernard's ability to participate in the political arena with all appropriateness necessary to impress and influence those in power. Yet despite the political overtones in many of these letters, Bernard was able to accomplish this without compromising his ecclesiastical reforming mission. At times Bernard was surprisingly bold to members of the nobility, deriding them at times for their lack of faith or support of his own causes, even when the 'cause' seemed trivial or beyond his responsibilities.[25] Despite these indiscretions, his fundamental concern for

24. *Ep* 126; *SBOp* 7:309.

25. For example, in a letter to Count Henry, son of Theobald, Bernard gives a strong warning from God if Henry does not replace the pigs lost by one of his peasants. *Ep* 279;

these secular leaders remained their relationship with Christ. Bernard understood that the temporal power these royals possessed meant that few people dared to speak plainly to them about issues in their personal lives. Bernard displayed no such fear, for his concern was their spiritual well-being as he wrote with the authority of God. The emphasis that Bernard placed on the individual cannot be stressed enough. Indeed, to fully grasp Bernard's spirituality, one could argue that he a twelfth-century humanist—interested in the inner workings of what makes the individual fully human and fully God's.

Bernard wrote fewer than thirty letters to ordinary laypersons (not including the secular nobility). Not surprisingly, a majority of these letters concerned personal spiritual matters rather than the affairs of ecclesiastical politics. Bernard was careful to leave the dealings of the church with those who have control to enact reform. To common laypersons, Bernard wrote primarily about their spiritual commitments and discipline, including chastisement for not entering Clairvaux as promised. A few of the letters were written to parents of sons who entered the Cistercian Order, either to console or condemn them for interfering in their sons' call to the monastic life.

Compared to his contemporaries, Bernard wrote a surprisingly large number of letters to women. He seems to have had no aversion to them, and was certainly not a misogynist. While his letters to female members of the secular nobility were primarily political in nature, Bernard wrote to nuns, abbesses, and other women with a decidedly spiritual tone. Eight of these letters were letters of encouragement and counsel. Ten letters seem to have been business letters, such as the letters to Melisande, the queen of Jerusalem.[26] These letters to Melisande alone serve as evidence that Bernard may have seen women as capable agents of change.[27] Had the saint seen women as a gender unequal to men in the eyes of God, then the content of these letters would have been dramatically different. A final set of letters to women of are letters of friendship, as in his letters to Beatrice[28] and

---

SBOp 8:191. Other examples of letters in this genre are *Ep* 97; *SBOp* 7:247–48 and *Ep* 128; *SBOp* 7:321–22.

26. *Ep* 206; *SBOp* 8:65, *Ep* 289; *SBOp* 8:205–06, *Ep* 354; *SBOp* 8:297–98, *Ep* 355; *SBOp* 8:299.

27. Krahmer, "Interpreting the Letters of Bernard of Clairvaux to Ermengarde," 231.

28. *Ep* 118; *SBOp* 7:298–99.

Ermengarde.[29] In his letters, Bernard treated women with the same respect he treated men (some might argue that the saint is far more cordial to his female recipients than he is to some of the men to whom he writes). The value that Bernard placed on the role of women in the work of Christ in the world differs from that of others in his time. He was not afraid of the potential scandal of writing to women, even letters as intimate as those to Ermengarde.

BERNARD'S EPISTOLARY OBJECTIVES

Bernard did not simply compose and compile his corpus of letters at random. Like most everything else he did, the saint had an agenda. He knew his letters would be read by many people, influencing more than just the persons to whom they were addressed. By looking at both the letter recipients and the general content, we can discern basic objectives that Bernard could have had in mind when composing his many epistles.

POLITICAL INTERESTS

Bernard understood and accepted the presence of the political system in the church, although at times he criticized those whose sole purpose (in Bernard's opinion) was to use political connections to gain stature and powerful appointments in the church. For example, one of Bernard's primary objections to the anti-pope Anacletus II and his supporters was that their motives were politically selfish, not having the best interests of the church in mind. He contrasted the motives of the anti-pope supporters with that of the followers of Innocent II, who rejected Anacletus "with one accord, with no inducement of money, undeceived by any fallacy, not led by considerations of human relationship, nor under duress from the civil power."[30] This statement clearly was an implicit indictment of the actions of the Anacletus supporters without explicitly accusing them of such behavior.

While Bernard did not particularly embrace the selfishness of political activity in the church, he never shied away from using it. He wrote dozens of letters to those with whom he had political favor, in support of either his own causes or the needs of others. The letters of Bernard, then, cannot be

29. *Ep* 116, 117; *SBOp* 7:296–97.
30. *Ep* 126; *SBOp* 7:316–17.

seen apart from this political connection. Bernard understood his letters as a form of sanctified political activity, for in Bernard's mind his letters or causes were never self-focused, but rather written for the sake of Christ and his church.

THEOLOGICAL ISSUES

Although Bernard was in many ways perfectly suited to the twelfth-century, he found himself increasingly alienated from many in the church regarding the new scholasticism of the time. As the twelfth-century progressed, scholasticism engaged the curious student who desired to know more than what the traditional commentaries of the church Fathers allowed. Bernard was obviously not among this group, which included Peter Abelard, his student Arnold of Brescia, and others. In his letters condemning Abelard's teachings, Bernard remained concise and straightforward in his criticisms. In no less than five letters criticizing the teacher, Bernard portrays Abelard as one who advocates, among other things, anti-trinitarianism. He even compares Abelard to heretics Arius, Pelagius, and Nestorius.

Bernard's letters contained far more theological issues than merely criticism of Abelard's teachings. Throughout his letters he dealt with (among other topics) Mariology,[31] baptism,[32] the Lord's Supper,[33] the concept of loving God,[34] human anthropology,[35] and worship.[36] Bernard would not want to be considered a scholastic theologian, however. His theology was in line with the church Fathers, and he believed that to seek theological knowledge for curiosity's sake was pride and had no place in the life of a monk. If studying theology did not lead to love, then it was a theology of pride.[37] However, to argue that Bernard did not believe that the practice of theology was an important venture is to misread the saint. His work *On Grace and Free Choice* is a clear example of medieval scholasticism at its

31. *Ep* 174; *SBOp* 7:388–92.
32. *Ep* 403; *SBOp* 8:383–84.
33. *Epp* 35–36; *SBOp* 7:92–94.
34. *Ep* 11; *SBOp* 7:52–60.
35. *Ep* 87; *SBOp* 7:224–31.
36. *Ep* 398; *SBOp* 8:377–79.

37. This is the case in the often-quoted paragraph from the *Song of Songs*, in which Bernard describes the difference between a humble and a prideful search for knowledge. *SC* 36; *SBOp* 2:5.

finest. Bernard's presentation in this work is well argued and arranged in a methodical and logical manner. While Bernard did not focus all his energies on scholastic pursuits, this work demonstrates that the saint clearly had the capacity to do so. His purpose was to create a theology that could potentially lead individuals to a mystical union with Christ.

APPROACH AND RATIONALE OF THE PRESENT STUDY

The large number of letters in Bernard's epistolary corpus makes a thorough study of them a daunting task. An examination of the spiritual direction in every letter would be fruitful, but is beyond the scope of this study. One method to examine the letters would be through analyzing them using representative letters and by classifying them by type. However, Bernard's letters can be organized several ways, including theme, genre, character, style, and date. The danger would be the creation of artificial theme constructions.[38]

The most logical approach to examining the letters of Bernard of Clairvaux utilizing a representative approach is by organizing them by recipient. The classification of his letters by recipient allows us to examine the saint's agenda for every people group in his society. It demonstrates the breadth of Bernard's epistolary influence, and the unique approach he uses for each culture. Therefore, our approach is to devote a chapter to each of the following groups of letter recipients: monks, abbots, bishops, popes, and the laity. Bernard was not diffident about sharing his schema of church reform. Regardless of the life situation of the recipients of his letters, Bernard wrote as one who knew God's plan for them. He maintained that all Christians could take part of God's purposes on earth, so the recipients of his letters are from a diverse collection of people groups.

The process of selecting letters from each category of people proved to be the most difficult task of this study, for each letter has evidence of a master rhetorical artisan at work, and to eliminate a single masterful letter is a crime. I have attempted to choose letters from each recipient group that best represents the saint's approach to the group as a whole. For example, my selection of letters to Pope Eugenius III includes letters that embody Bernard's agenda for the Cistercian pontiff. His letters to Suger, abbot of St. Denis represent Bernard's desire to influence the political abbot while King Louis VII was away on the Second Crusade. While this approach is

38. Constable, *Letters and Letter-Collections*, 23.

not a perfect method, I believe it to be both reliable and faithful to this charismatic Cistercian leader and his agenda for the church.

For the sake of consistency with most Bernardine scholars, I have retained the letter numbering of the critical edition. As for the examination of the selected letters, my approach is an inductive exegesis, allowing Bernard's text to speak for itself; placed in the context of the letter itself, the epistolary corpus, and Bernard's understanding of himself and the world around him. Woven throughout the exegetical work with the letters are insights into Bernard's theology, anthropology, and reformational zeal.

CHAPTER 4

The Letters of Bernard to Monks

BERNARD BELIEVED THE MONASTIC vocation held such an important place in the heart of God and in the church that he argued that monastic discipline deserved the right to be called a "second baptism." According to Bernard, a monastic life is the surest way to heaven, but it is not a guarantee. He likened heaven to being on the other side of a lake. While the layperson must swim across, the monk can walk across a bridge of holiness. However, this holy life must manifest itself in a life faithful to the Benedictine vows of stability, conversion of manners, and obedience. To Bernard, the greatest advantage of a monastic life is that the monk could always hear the voice of Christ; however, his voice was not always heard through books, for it is easier to heed Christ's exhortations by following him than by reading about him.

In his letters, Bernard compares earthly Jerusalem to those called to a religious life who imitate as far as they can the ways of the heavenly Jerusalem.[1] Monks should always be near the place where Christ died, and for Bernard this could be anywhere. The spiritual Jerusalem is a place far removed from sin and society but close to God and God's angels. The earthly Jerusalem was the place Christ went to die for the eternal benefit of humanity. For the monk, the spiritual Jerusalem is a place they enter to die to themselves for the glory of Christ and his Bride, the church. Of course, according to its proud abbot, the abbey of Clairvaux, built on piety, self-sacrifice, and Christian charity, was itself the true Jerusalem, free from the clutches of political powers and Muslim influence. Clairvaux is Jerusalem

---

1. *SC* 55.2; *SBOp* 1:112.

in that she is "one with the Jerusalem in heaven, in whole-hearted devotion in the mind, in similarity of life, and in spiritual kinship."[2]

The monastic community for Bernard was a Trinitarian communion. In their lives together, monks lived in a mysterious grace, following the example of the Trinitarian nature of God, in which their very social community was a unifying communion with both themselves and with the inner life of God. The monastery was a model for the entire church, which should follow the monks' dependence upon God, commitment to obedience, and faithfulness to Christ. By uniting themselves to Christ, monks were serving both themselves and others, for they are united to the whole the church, called to watch over the whole church and be spiritually responsible for all in the whole church.

Would an abbot of a monk who received a letter from Bernard have felt threatened? The abbot could have assumed that Bernard was involving himself in the dealings of the abbot's abbey. However, medieval letters were anything but private. They were public documents written with the assumption that many people would read them. Individual privacy in medieval Europe was rare. A monk receiving a letter from Bernard would have to expect that his abbot would have read it, particularly if the monk, due to illiteracy or blindness, could not read the letter himself.

The importance of Bernard's letters to monks lies in their monastic theology. Through these letters, Bernard reveals his ideals for a renewed monasticism in the church. The hidden-ness of monks and their humble place in the church gave them the opportunity to exist as selfless servants of Christ, called to deny their lives for the sake of God. For Cistercian monks, Bernard held an even higher standard. God called these monks not simply to a hidden life, but a life of austere physical conditions that would lead them to Christ for consolation. However, as this chapter will demonstrate, not all monks shared the abbot's enthusiasm for Cistercian hardships and strict obedience. Despite occasional apathy on the part of monks for Bernard's monastic ideals, the abbot's sincere interest in the spiritual state of these monks is evident in these letters.

---

2. *Ep* 64.2; *SBOp* 7:158.

LETTER 1 TO ROBERT (1125)[3]

Written in 1125, this letter was actually Bernard's first definitive statement regarding Cistercian renewal in contrast to that of Cluny. When Robert was a child, his parents oblated him to Cluny. However, influenced by the charisma of his cousin Bernard, Robert joined the Cistercians, first at Cîteaux, and later at Clairvaux. However, the severe Cistercian life was not appealing to Robert. In 1119, while Bernard was isolated from the community to recover from an illness, Robert left Clairvaux with a representation from Cluny. Bernard, knowing of the infant Robert's oblation to Cluny, was not surprised, but was obviously outraged that the Cluniacs would enter Clairvaux and snatch one of his sheep. While this long letter implores Robert to return to Clairvaux, it also serves as an important document regarding Bernard's monastic theology. Much of the letter contains aspects of a court trial, with Cluny serving as the defendant, Bernard as the prosecutor, and Christ as the judge.

The structure of the thirteen-section letter is quite straightforward:

> 1) Opening Statements (Paragraphs 1–3)
>
> 2) The Crime (Paragraphs 4–6)
>
> 3) The Case (Paragraphs 7–9)
>
> 4) Closing Arguments (Paragraphs 10–13)

Opening Statements (Par. 1–3)

Bernard begins the letter by regretting that Robert has left freedom for bondage. On the surface, this statement is quite interesting, since a life at Cluny might afford more personal freedoms than the strict life in Clairvaux. However, Bernard's concern is Robert's spiritual bondage, and the abbot expresses his grief, sorrow, and anxiety for his cousin's soul. Although Robert's body would have more freedoms in Cluny than at Clairvaux, his soul would be imprisoned.

Bernard states he does not want to dwell on why Robert left, but rather why he will not return. The abbot acknowledges that Robert may have left, in fact, due to the abbot's strictness and severity with him. Bernard admits

---

3. The dating of many of Bernard's letters are an approximation. Scholars have deduced the time of their composition based on historical content and context. For letters without a composition year listed, the date is unknown.

that he is sorry for the way he treated Robert, but maintains that while he was strict with him, he was not malicious. He writes, "You will discover that I have been changed as you have been changed, and whereas before you feared me as a master, you will now embrace me freely as a companion."

Bernard enhances his supplication that Robert return. He writes, "I humble myself before you, I promise you of my love; and you are afraid? Be bold, and come where humility calls you and love draws you." Bernard's desire is to woo Robert back to Clairvaux as Jesus woos a sinner to his side. He offers counsel to Robert that he believes is in the best interest of Robert's soul. If Robert left Clairvaux out of fear, it will be love, and not condemnation that will encourage him to return. Bernard knows Robert and loves him more than anyone at Cluny ever could. He knows what is best for him: To return at once to Clairvaux, where the past difficulties would be behind them. Before them is a glorious future.

The Crime (Par. 4–6)

Bernard tells a parable of a "Grand Prior" sent by the chief of all the priors into the midst of some shepherds. Outside the prior looked like a sheep, but inwardly he was a wolf. Because he looked like a sheep, the shepherds admitted him into their fold. Once there, the prior began to preach a new gospel of feasting, sloth, talkativeness, and other actions that the shepherds had once tried to avoid. The wolf began to ask questions, such as, "Why would God make food if it was not to be eaten?" He tempted the shepherds and made them question their obligations and vows.

Bernard continues the story by describing a naïve boy being deceived by the ravenous Prior and taken to Cluny. Once there he is shaved, placed in silken robes and despite his youth, treated as royalty. To the others at Cluny he was treasure they had stolen. They cared not for the boy's conscience, but rather only for his physical presence with them. The consequences of this action are that Robert made a second profession without atoning for the transgression of breaking his Cistercian vow. The result is that, in the words of Romans 7:13, sin becomes sin above measure.

The Case (Par. 7–9)

At this point in the letter, the atmosphere of love, forgiveness, and forgetting the past that Bernard used to begin the letter is forgotten. For the next three paragraphs, the abbot speaks in harsh language of the judgment of Christ upon the sinful. At times Bernard seems to have forgotten that he is composing a letter to Robert, for he appeals to the Lord Jesus to intervene on his behalf. He directs his comments not to Robert, but to Christ, imploring the Almighty to remember how he labored and suffered on Robert's behalf, prayed day and night for him, and bore Robert's anxieties, troubles, and pain upon his own heart.

Seemingly leaving Robert behind, Bernard begins a third-person discussion of the issues involved, as if he is pacing a courtroom, addressing Christ, the Judge. "Let them see and judge which ought to be better to stand: either the vow a father makes for his son or a vow a son makes himself, especially when the son makes a much greater vow." In the argument that follows, Bernard argues to Christ that Cluny has no right to claim Robert. In fact, he alleges that Cluny desired not Robert, but the land that went to him at his supposed infant oblation.

Cluny is on trial, and Bernard is the prosecutor. Christ, the Righteous Judge, sits on his throne, hearing arguments from the litigators, although Cluny has no voice in these court proceedings. One cannot ignore the distinct possibility that the abbot was in actuality addressing the Cluniac leadership who would undoubtedly be reading this letter. Christ serves as a convenient third-person to whom Bernard can address his concerns without directly confronting those in Cluny. Bernard's language is sharply critical in this passage; ripe with resentment towards his Cluniac counterparts.

Suddenly, without any transition whatsoever, Bernard addresses Robert, calling him as a witness to his own actions. Bernard reminds his cousin that he begged to be admitted to Cîteaux, but was impeded until he was older. He reminds Robert that he was a novice for a year and then made a decision to make his profession. "O foolish boy!" the abbot exclaims. "Who has cast a spell on you to loosen the vow which adorned your lips?" He implores Robert to focus not on the vow his parents made but the vow that he himself made. Bernard encourages the young man to be on guard for those around him who might tempt him to ignore this counsel, shutting his ears to those who flatter him. Instead, he should search his own heart, for he knows himself best. Of course, Bernard knows what is best for Robert, and suggests that if Robert truly understood himself he would know that what Bernard is arguing is true.

CLOSING ARGUMENTS (PAR. 10–13)

In a reference to 1 Corinthians 4:14–15, Bernard turns from cross-examination to consolation: "I have said this, my son, not to upset you, but in order to admonish you as a precious son, because, although you have many masters in Christ, you have few fathers." Bernard is Robert's true spiritual father, for it was he who begot the young man in religion. As his true spiritual mother, Bernard nourished Robert with the milk of words. Had Robert stayed, he could have grown to feast on bread. Bernard expresses grief that when Robert left, the abbot felt like a mother whose child was taken from her, making her feel as if she has lost a part of herself.

Bernard reasons with Robert to consider why the monks of Cluny had done this. Was it for Robert's own benefit, or for themselves? The only desire Bernard has is the security of Robert's soul. If furs, soft cloth, and lavish meals made someone a saint, then why did Bernard not join him at Cluny? In a passage reminiscent of the *Apologia*, Bernard derides Cluny's generous use of spices, meats, and large meals, stating, "Frying pans do not fatten the soul." Idleness, he writes, makes one delicate. Hard work makes one hungry. If the monks of Cluny had truly cared for Robert's soul they would have left him where he might find the surest way to heaven.

Bernard closes the letter with a triumphant charge, reminiscent of 2 Timothy 2:3: "Arise, soldier of Christ, arise! Shake off the dust and return to the battle from whence you fled. You will fight more bravely after your flight, and you will triumph gloriously." Bernard's letter to Robert has come full-circle. What began as encouraging love to woo back a wayward son and continued as a threat of condemnation, has now found fulfillment in a rousing call to action to live a life of eternal, glorious bliss. Dying in battle is not death, but life, for after death he will be crowned. However, Bernard cannot close the letter without one final admonition. He warns Robert that if he reads this letter and does not respond favorably, his soul will be in peril at the last judgment. However, the decision is ultimately up to Robert as what he will choose to do. Bernard has offered spiritual counsel to Robert, who must now use his faculties of spiritual discretion in deciding his fate.

Despite the political consequences surrounding this situation with Robert (which certainly played a factor in the content of this letter), Bernard's primary concern was his cousin's spiritual well-being. He also felt regret for having been too harsh on the young man when he was at Clairvaux. Robert's personal ambition had tempted him to inquire about Cluny. His lack of obedience led him there. However, the situation was far more extensive than just being concerned with Robert. His cousin represented others in the church who were not faithful to their vocational calling. Their faithfulness would have consequences for the entire church.

LETTERS TO THE MONKS OF CLAIRVAUX

One must empathize with the monks of Clairvaux. While Bernard was their abbot in name, his absence and worldly distractions often diverted his attention from their spiritual needs and kept him away from Clairvaux for long periods. In all practicality, the Prior of Clairvaux was more of an abbot to the monks than was their famous founder. For those entered Clairvaux after being stirred by the abbot's motivational preaching, his absence must have been exceedingly difficult.

Bernard understood this dilemma, and at times expressed both guilt and regret for being away from them. He knew that according to Chapter 2 of the *Rule*, his primary duty as abbot was the spiritual direction of his monks. His role was to represent Christ to them and he would be held accountable on Judgment Day for his obedience to this task. Bernard's letters to his monks are some of the most intimate and revealing letters in the epistolary corpus. Through them, he attempts to rationalize his frequent absences, and endeavors to console their longing hearts.

LETTER 143 (1135)

The significance of this letter seems to stem from an early vocational conflict in Bernard. Although he feels an obligation to intercede on behalf of the papal schism, he also bears the weight of the spiritual upbringing of his monastic sons. In the letter, Bernard assumes that his monks long for his presence and reassures them that he must be doing God's work away from Clairvaux.

In this very emotional and intimate letter, written around 1135, Bernard expresses his longing for his brothers at Clairvaux and encourages them to continue living faithfully to God. He addresses the letter to "monks, lay-brothers, and novices," indicating the existence of three distinct groups within the Clairvaux community. Ordering the recipients the way he does may indicate a spiritual hierarchy. Bernard lists the monks first because they have made a solemn profession and live in the cloister. The lay brothers are listed second because they have professed to follow the lay-brother statues. He lists novices last because they have not yet made a profession of any kind.

Interestingly, he begins by informing them how deeply *he* is suffering because he is away from them. The abbot knows that his absence is not popular among his monks, and to quell their selfish longing for him, he directs their attention to him and his longing to be with them. He shares that while they yearn for just one person, he yearns for each one of them, which is a much greater burden than they have. "Knowing this," he writes, "my delay is not my desire, but is necessary for the church; so you ought not to be angry with me, but have compassion for me." He reminds them that he is suffering for God, and since they long for his presence, they are suffering for God with him. Since they are all suffering together, they should rejoice, because God is with them both, which means that spiritually they are united in him. Since the suffering of Christ on the cross was directed towards his glorification, followers of Christ must endeavor to suffer with Christ. Human suffering directs our attention on the prize of heaven, where faithful Christians will ascend. This separation between Bernard and his monks will lead them to seek solace in the suffering and exaltation of Christ. Although they are separated by geography, they are united in Christ's suffering.

Bernard tempers this unification in Christ, however, with an admonition reminiscent of Psalm 1. He writes that not everyone in Clairvaux may be united to him. Those who are humble, reverent, devoted to reading, vigilant in prayer, and concerned with brotherly love can be assured that they are near to his heart. However, those who are scheming, double-faced, murmuring, rebellious, insubordinate, restless and wandering, and who unblushingly eat the bread of idleness, are far from him, even if Bernard happened to be standing beside them at Clairvaux. Bernard uses this opportunity to teach them as if they were in daily chapter listening to his spiritual instruction. The faithfulness of each monk affects the faithfulness of the entire Clairvaux community.

Through this letter, Bernard is offering his monks an opportunity to shepherd their abbot through their prayers and empathy. Rather than demonstrating stoicism, he appears vulnerable and honest in his emotions. This approach demonstrates to the monks of Clairvaux that although they are the spiritual sons, their spiritual father is not without needs. In their commitment to each other, mutual accountability and humility are means to faithful Christian community. The ministry they have to offer their abbot is a life of prayer, which results from their faith, hope, and thankfulness.

The close of this letter contains an exhortation for the community to maintain a three-fold service to God until he returns. First, they are to serve God with fear, so that when they are delivered from the enemy they may serve him without fear. Fear of God stuns us, but it does not save us. Secondly, they are to serve God with hope, because God is faithful. However, hope is only for learners in Christ, not the perfect. Therefore, they are to serve God with integrity, because God has a claim on it. Integrity is a pure love for God through which one might confidently approach God's throne.

Although he is far away from them, attempting to keep the church together in the midst of the papal schism, he has not forgotten his obligation as their spiritual father. They are his children and his brothers, and he cares for them. They should not feel sorry for themselves that he is gone, but rather follow his example by serving God with love. "I serve him willingly, because love sets me free." With these words, he closes the letter; knowing that despite their isolation from each other, their bond will be God's love.

Bernard defense of his presence away from his monastery indicates that he wanted to make it perfectly clear to his monks that his absence did not result from personal ambition, but obedience to the church. Since he would rather be with them rather than where he was, his travels on behalf of the Roman pontiff was a spiritual lesson to them of obedience to Christ. As he was serving the Pope submissively, so should they comply with his wishes in serving Christ humbly while he was away from them.

Letter 144 (1137)

Letter 144, written two years after the previous letter, was also sent to his monks while Bernard was away on church business. However, the letter's content and style are vastly different from *Letter 143*. While in the former letter Bernard prides himself on his obedience to the pope, in this letter he bemoans that obedience. "My soul is sorrowful," he writes, "and will not be consoled until I have returned to you." He refers to himself in exile, and the mere thought of his monks is his only consolation. Although this remark is probably hyperbolic, that Bernard would make such a statement (and not rephrase it later for the letter collection) demonstrates the honesty of the abbot and the deep understanding he has of himself. At this moment in his life, not even God can bring consolation—only his monks.

He laments how this is the third time he has been torn away from his children who have had to be weaned before they were ready. He has been forced to leave his own to care for the needs of others. This suffering is too painful to bear. "Lord, it is better for me to die than it is to live," he writes. His sons would be better served without him. He prays that God would let his monks close his eyes and lay his broken-hearted body in the ground. Bernard comes dangerously close to self-pity in this section of the letter, for the focus of his concern is his own consolation through grief. However, since he writes that his death would benefit his monks, his concerns are ultimately for them.

While grief has overcome him, Bernard still has the ability to relate that his efforts have produced some fruit, although he admits he is too humble to share the details of how his presence has been beneficial. Despite his personal anguish, God is still at work through him. He has laid his sickly, broken body down for God, and God has chosen to use his efforts.

Bernard closes the letter with some news of his activities, although in the midst of them he has been "terrified by the phantom of pale death." In an example of obedience and faithfulness, he has submitted himself to the Emperor, the Pope, to the prayers of the church, and to the secular princes and allowed himself to be dragged to Apulia, where he had to confront the violent Roger of Sicily. He asks them to pray for peace in the church, to pray for his health, and, in a reversal of attitude from earlier in the letter, to pray that he will be able to see them again, live with them, and finally die with them. He exhorts them to "live that your prayers might avail." After lamenting once again over his forsaken place in the world and failing health, he presses them once again to pray for him, for the Pope, and for others who are with him, which includes his brother Gerard.

The Bernard of this letter is far different from the fiery champion of Innocent II found in other letters. While the tone of *Letter 143* is that of Bernard wanting the Clairvaux community to respect him for his absence, in reading this letter it seems that Bernard was actually describing his own desperation and inner agony. How this letter was received at Clairvaux is unknown, but in a letter such as this, the saintly abbot would have appeared very human to his monks, allowing them to empathize with him in his loneliness and grief. In Bernard's letter to Robert, he acknowledges that Robert feared him for his asceticism and holiness. In his human frailty and vulnerability, Bernard the abbot, the mediator, the reformer, and the future saint became Bernard the brother who needed the support and prayers of others. This approachability of his character seems to be missing in his earlier years. The Bernard of 1137 had grown to realize that he needed others, and he was asking for help. This act alone served as an example of implicit spiritual direction to his monks. The appearance of humility and acknowledging the need for help exemplifies the qualities of Cistercian monk.[4]

LETTERS TO THE MONK ADAM

The letters to Adam originated from a somewhat embarrassing situation for the Cistercians. Sometime in 1124, Arnold, the abbot of Morimond, decided on his own initiative to make a monastic foundation in the Holy Land. He resigned his abbacy and recruited several monks to go with him. This scandalous action was amplified even more considering that Arnold, Morimond's founding abbot, came from a powerful family in Germany, and was viewed by the Cistercians as an able leader. When word spread that Arnold had made such a decision without the consent of the General Chapter, the Cistercians attempted to encourage their wayward brother to return. As a new monastic Order with the novel idea of a governing, annual General Chapter, the Cistercians desired to be viewed as a legitimate Order by others in the church. This scandal with Arnold must have made the Cistercians look particularly unorganized and lacking control over their monasteries.

These letters to Adam, one of the monks accompanying the prodigal abbot, exemplify Bernard's theology of communal obedience, particularly with regard to the fledgling Cistercian movement. In Bernard's mind, the mystical union between Christ and the church is so deep that the two do not exist without one another. Because Christians are united to Christ through the church, this mystical marriage is not for their own good but for the good of others. As Jean Leclercq states, Bernard understood Christians as "united to all, called on to watch over all, and consequently responsible for all."[5] Although people lived in communities, whether abbeys, cities, or rural villages, their true citizenship was in heaven, and people in all areas of life should strive to live in such a manner as to reflect this citizenship, as the church is the divine norm of national identity.[6]

4. In fact, the argument can be made that in this letter, particularly chapters 2 and 7, Bernard was exhibiting the *Rule* before his monks.

5. Leclercq, "Contemplative Community," 97–112.

6. Williams, "The Political Philosophy of Saint Bernard of Clairvaux," 466–69.

The early order of Citeaux desired to live as a faithful Spouse by carefully following St. Benedict's *Rule*. The Cistercians' emphasis on poverty, asceticism, simplicity in art and architecture, and ordinary lifestyle was a mere function of their devotion to Christ. Breaking from traditional monastic customs, the Cistercians set themselves apart from other orders (even the new orders). They were obsessed with the *puritas Regulae* and desired none other than to follow Christ through a judicious following of its text.

Of course, this means of following Christ made an implicit commentary on other monastic orders that had a more open understanding of Benedict. For the early Cistercians, the monastery, more than a school of learning, was a school of charity.[7] This understanding caused many to view the Cistercians as pious, prideful monks who only knew humility in the context of comparing themselves to other. The situation with Arnold and his monk had the potential of severely affecting Cistercian order and morale, not to mention its legitimacy. Bernard felt the need to address the situation himself as the spokesperson of the Order.

LETTER 5 (1124)

Abbot Arnold died before they reached Jerusalem. One monk, Adam, emerged as their new leader. Bernard wrote *Letter 5* before he had heard of Abbot Arnold's death. In the letter, he scolds the monk for following his abbot on the unlawful pilgrimage after Adam had assured Bernard that he would not. Apparently, this pilgrimage was not a surprise, but an endeavor that Arnold had planned for some time. Bernard, aware of Arnold's restlessness, attempted in vain to thwart him in his plans. The letter begins with a stern rebuke. Since Bernard knows the humility and integrity of Adam's heart, he feels compelled to address him more sharply and rebuke him more freely than he would have if he did not know Adam very well.

Bernard's primary concern for Adam is twofold. First, the monk has lost all sense.[8] Second, he believes that Adam has descended into this state because he has allowed the Tempter to delude his mind. He reminds Adam not to believe every spirit he encounters. He should learn from King Solomon, who had many friends, but only one in a thousand was his counselor. Bernard cites passages from scripture that might teach Adam to have a more discerning spirit. For example, if he continues in his current path, his

---

7. Bamberger, "The Monastic Vision of Saint Bernard of Clairvaux," 46–58.

8. Bernard calls him *insensate*; *Ep* 5; *SBOp* 7:28.

house will be built on sand, not on the rock of Christ (Matt 7:26). Adam's very salvation was at risk.

Since Bernard has respect for Adam, and despite the monk's poor judgment, he agrees to meet with him to resolve the matter. "I implore you by the bowels of Christ's mercy," Bernard writes, "That you will by no means depart, or at least you could come to a convenient place for us to talk." Bernard's desire is to see what can be done to remedy Adam from all the evil that Bernard fears has come to him. God's grace abounds in this letter, though Bernard disguises it in an attempt to get Adam's attention.

Although Bernard states at the start of the letter that his language would be harsh, in reality his language is one of concern, not rebuke. Certainly, he uses much harsher language in other letters (including *Letter 1* to his cousin Robert). Bernard sees potential in Adam, and desires not to drive him away but to help him become restored to the Order and to God through this intentional spiritual counsel.

Letter 7 (1125)

When word reached Clairvaux of Abbot Arnold's death, Bernard sent Adam a second letter. Much longer than his first letter, this letter seems almost more of a treatise on monastic obedience than a letter.[9] Adam had emerged as the leader of the wayward monks, and Bernard wrote to encourage him to return to Morimond. The letter is a methodical, carefully worded document that demonstrates the irrationality of following their abbot and the necessity of returning to their monastery.

The letter begins with Bernard's reminder to Adam that he and his band are not an isolated community, but part of a much larger fellowship of brothers, beginning with those in Morimond and extending to the entire Cistercian Order. Since they have offended their monastic brothers, Adam and the other monks must seek reconciliation. Bernard argues why the monks should not have followed their abbot. Although Adam and the other monks thought they were being obedient in following their abbot, now that he is dead, they have no obligation to him but to the Order. Since he is dead, the abbot asks, "Why are you hesitating to correct this great scandal?" The solution is quite simple: All Adam has to do is lead the monks home.

The abbot puts forth a logical theological argument that even though Adam and the others left with Abbot Arnold because he commanded them

---

9. Some manuscripts refer to this letter as, *Of Discernment in Obedience.*

to go, disobeying the Divine in order to be obedient to a human is *perversum*. He argues that some things, such as faith, hope, and charity, are always good, and we should never forbid doing them. Some things are always evil, such as theft, sacrilege, and adultery, which we should never do. Furthermore, some things are in the middle, neither good nor evil, such as fasting, vigils, and reading. To these things, obedience is never wrong. However, people can use these middle things for either good or evil. For example, marriage is good, but dissolving the marriage is evil. Another example regards the ownership of property. For a secular person to own property is neither good nor evil, but for a monk it is completely evil.

Bernard then asks Adam if he can yet decipher in which of these divisions his leaving Morimond belongs. Rather than being either good or evil, he states the action might be excused on the grounds of obedience to an abbot, but the delay in returning cannot be excused. If Arnold had commanded them to do something he should not have done, now that he is dead Adam should not obey him any longer. Bernard's logic makes Adam's decision to follow Arnold seem foolish, comparing his actions to the Psalmist's description of one who consorts with thieves and adulterers. "[Arnold] has disregarded his superiors, he has abandoned his subordinates, and he has upset his brothers; and you, seeing the thief, ran with him?"

Bernard then moves from Adam's actions to his conscience. Did he set out from his monastery willingly or unwillingly? He asks this because if he set out willingly, then it was not from obedience, making his actions evil. If he was unwilling, then he should have known by his conscience that the abbot's actions were questionable. Either way, Adam had no excuse for leaving with his abbot. If he questioned the abbot's decision to leave, then he should have followed Cistercian regulations and called an inquiry. Bernard demonstrates the folly of Adam's decision: "Tell me then, I ask, were [your abbot] to put a sword in your hand, and then order you to cut his throat, would you do it?" In a sin of omission, he did not call forth an inquiry, but rather followed his abbot. The result is he has murdered his abbot's soul.

The remainder of the letter is a teaching of the meaning of monastic obedience. Adam's vow to obedience was not just to his abbot, or to the Cistercian Order, but to Almighty God himself. The Rule of Benedict is the means by which monks stay obedient to God. This obedience includes the vow of stability, which is so important that even if an angel of heaven were to command Bernard to do something contrary to this, he would not follow the order for fear of being a perjurer before God. Adam's blunder is that while he should have known, he did not understand the meaning of monastic obedience.

This interpretation of obedience is clear in Bernard: A Cistercian's first obedience is not to the *Rule*, but to the law of God. An abbot is not above the *Rule*, but is himself a monk living in obedience to the *Rule*. In this instance, Adam's disobedience stemmed from his perceived obedience to his erring abbot. Bernard stresses to Adam that obedience to God begins with obedience to oneself, and self-obedience grows from self-knowledge. Had Adam understood himself in relation to his abbot and to God, he would not have found himself in his present situation.

At the conclusion of the letter, Bernard warns Adam that he holds in his hands the fates of all the renegade monks with him. If they do not return with him, Adam has the authority to excommunicate them.[10] The implicit warning to Adam is that if he himself does not return, Bernard would excommunicate him (that Bernard actually had the authority to excommunicate Adam is highly doubtful!). This is a strong way to end the letter, but the abbot wants Adam to understand the gravity of this situation. Adam was being called to obey Bernard or else face dire spiritual consequences.

What makes this lengthy letter interesting is that unlike other letters Bernard wrote to individuals with whom he was disappointed, his customary emotionalism is absent. Instead, he demonstrates his ability to set forth a fact-laden, logical argument. He undoubtedly knew that Adam had the capacity to follow such an argument. Once again, Bernard patterns his rhetorical method to suit the recipient of the letter. He had a remarkable ability to communicate with many different personality and intellectual types, and he knew what style would solicit the response he desired. In this instance, his method was successful, for Adam and his monks returned and were restored. According to Leclercq, Adam later became the first abbot of Ebrach, a Morimond foundation in Germany.

---

10. The legality of Adam's ability to excommunicate is doubtful. Acting under the authority of his bishop, Bernard could pronounce excommunication. Bernard granted Adam the authority to excommunication under proxy, despite the fact that the excommunication would likely not be valid, since Bernard did not have direct authority over Adam and his monks.

LETTER 142 TO THE MONKS OF THE ABBEY IN THE ALPS (1138)

The abbey of St. Jean-d'Aulps affiliated with Clairvaux in 1136. It began as a small community of reforming monks in 1090 who left Molesme to found a new community. They initially settled in the diocese of Besançon, but then moved into the diocese of Geneva. In 1138, their abbot Garin was elected Bishop of Sion (Sitten) in the Rhone valley.

The significance of this letter is that it demonstrates Bernard's view of himself as an abbot of more than Clairvaux. He uses the occasion of this letter (the loss of their abbot to the episcopacy) to influence their election of someone who would reflect his own monastic ideals. Bernard reminds them to remain where they are, and not to be tempted to leave during this volatile transition of leadership. While their abbot has been raised to a higher place, they are called to remain hidden and humble. He praises the monks for sharing the holy life of their abbot with the world. This act not only makes their own lives more holy, but they have proved themselves humble by staying where they are.

For Bernard, ambition is the opposite of pride.[11] In praising the monks for their stability, Bernard stresses their obedience. Humility begins with obedience to oneself, which in turn leads to vocational obedience. This twofold obedience results in obedience to Christ. The monks' abbot was obedient in heeding the call to the episcopacy. They should follow his example by staying obedient to their vocational calling to monastic seclusion.

In the second paragraph of the letter, Bernard explains the essence of their holiness and humility. He writes, "This virtue, in my opinion, is to be preferred to prolonged fasts and planned vigils, indeed to all bodily exercise . . ." He reminds them that who they are is far more important that what they do. Their calling is not to do the work of a monk, but rather to possess the virtues of a monk. Bernard is stressing the mystical concept of "being" over "doing" in finding one's identity and vocation. Although Bernard certainly believed that godliness is to be achieved by actively doing the work of God, he clearly believes that the essence of Christian virtue is developed internally, rather than externally. Virtue is the essence of unity in Christ, as well, for faithfulness is achieved in community. The faithfulness of the whole is made possible by the faithfulness of the individual.

---

11. In his treatise to Henry, Archbishop of Sens, Bernard argues that the only acceptable ambition is the zeal for spiritual gain. *Ep* 42; *SBOp* 7:123.

Bernard closes the letter with an exhortation to elect an abbot expeditiously. He writes, "Invoke the Holy Spirit and then hurry up and elect your father." He encourages them to do this hastily in order to bring stability and order to the abbey. Prayer should never be procrastinated. The most effective means of electing an abbot is through prayer, appealing to the Holy Spirit for guidance. The virtue he exhorts them to manifest and the prayers he encourages them to offer will affect the outcome of their abbatial election. Holiness of heart and life leads to one's prayers having more meaning, for the more virtuous the life, the deeper one's prayers will be. Once again, Bernard is stressing the synthesis between the ecclesiastic and the personal. His only counsel regarding whom to choose is that they "choose so great a person that he would have in his mind the honor of God, and your salvation." This is no mere election. It will have eternal consequences, so they should choose well.

LETTER 154 TO BERNARD, MONK OF THE CHARTREUSE-DES-PORTES-EN-BUGEY (1136)

In this short letter, Bernard mentions the initiation his *Sermons on the Song of Songs*. While this alone does not seem to fall into the category of *spiritual direction*, it demonstrates Bernard's desire for confirmation from others. The epistle is written to a Carthusian monk to whom Bernard had made a promise to visit. Hindered by his many affairs, Bernard had not been able to fulfill his pledge. However, Bernard has been able to fulfill the monk's other request that the abbot of Clairvaux compose some sermons for him on the beginning of the Song of Songs, which he sends with the letter. Bernard requests that the monk read the sermons and then recommend whether or not he should continue writing them. He writes that as soon as he is able, the monk "should write back and advise if they should be continued or stopped."

This letter demonstrates the honesty Bernard had with himself. Not wanting simply to compose the sermons of his own volition or ambition, he sought the counsel of a person at a lower ecclesiastical level than he was. Bernard desired to be obedient to Christ. By seeking counsel and accountability from another, he confirmed his desire to write the sermons. Interpreting sacred scripture was not an individual right, but a responsibility for and with the entire faith community. The purpose behind Bernard's desire to compose the sermon series is unknown. However, with an affinity towards the church Fathers, he may have wanted to secure his place in the interpretational tradition of Origen, Gregory the Great, Jerome, Bede, and others. Although Bernard desired to interpret the Song of Songs in his own way, he would not have wanted to disagree with these church Fathers, an act that had brought scandal to Peter Abelard. By writing *Letter 154*, the abbot wanted others to know that he was beginning the sermons. By seeking divine direction through others, he demonstrated humility and obedience to God.[12]

LETTER 322 TO HUGH, A NOVICE (1138)

Hugh, possibly a novice at the Cistercian abbey of Miroir, seems to have come from the nobility. Bernard had hoped for and expected the young man's conversion, and wrote this very practical letter to congratulate and encourage him in his novitiate. The abbot praises young Hugh for his courageous actions. He tells Hugh that although he is delicate of body, he has conquered the evil one, despised the world, forsaken his body, rejected the affection of his relatives, and like the eagle described in Isaiah 40, has taken wing on a spiritual flight.

Bernard, also raised as a noble, offers the young monk some practical counsel. "Do not let the roughness of our Order frighten your tender life," he writes. Instead, he reminds Hugh to remember that the sweetness of Christ present with him will season the bitterness of the prophet's flour. Should Hugh feel the sting of temptation, he should gaze upon the church's crucifix, which like the serpent on the staff in the desert, will act as the instrument of God to restore him to spiritual health.

One interesting aspect of this letter is Bernard's metaphor of Jesus as a sacrificing mother. He encourages Hugh to look to Jesus when he feels weak, for Jesus is his true mother. Jesus, like a mother, laid down his life for his children. Hugh must also be willing to lay down his life for Christ, allowing the nails of Christ to pass through his own hands and feet. In fact, Bernard extends this concept to portray Jesus as Hugh's true mother. The abbot quotes *Letter 14* of Jerome to Heliodorus, a former soldier who had left a life of desert asceticism for a less severe clerical position in the city. Jerome chides Heliodorus that no one, not even his father prostrated over the threshold nor his weeping mother exposing the breasts that once fed him,

12. Whether or not Bernard received permission from the abbot of Cîteaux (his superior) is unknown.

should keep him from following Christ, his true Parent.[13] Bernard reminds the young monk not to weep for his earthly parents, for they do not understand that he has been transformed from a child of wrath to a child of God. In fact, he exhorts Hugh not to listen to anyone from his extended family or even his Cistercian family who tries to make Hugh believe that he was too young to enter the monastery. Instead of focusing on what others say, he should focus on being obedient to Christ, his true Parent. "Farewell, and strive to persevere," Bernard concludes the letter, "For only perseverance is crowned." This final statement reflects Bernard's understanding of the largest obstacle in Hugh's life. By offering this counsel, the abbot leaves Hugh with a challenge and an encouragement to complete what he has begun in his spiritual journey.

LETTER 414 TO ALARD, THE MONK

At times Bernard found himself at the center of a Cistercian family altercation. This controversy came from Foigny Abbey, a daughter house of Clairvaux founded in 1121. While their abbot, Rainald, was away, a certain monk named Alard instigated trouble against a novice named Adamarus, who was eventually expelled from the monastery. The novice made his way to Clairvaux, where Bernard counseled, encouraged, and sent him back to Foigny.[14] These monks were not strangers to Bernard, and his involvement in this situation is not surprising. As the abbot of Foigny's motherhouse, the abbot had frequent contacts with their affairs, and he would have felt responsible for the overall health of the abbey.

In *Letter 414*, Bernard addresses Alard directly. From the very way Bernard introduces himself in the letter, Alard could decipher the tone of what would follow. "To his beloved son Alard, from Brother Bernard: paternal love and affection." This letter is a spiritual father directing a spiritual son, but the father also acknowledges that he himself is still the son's brother. The very means with which Bernard words the salutation serves to disarm any defensive attitude Alard might have in receiving a scolding letter from a spiritual father. He was writing with authority, but as a loving father and fellow monk so Alard might know that he genuinely cares for him.

---

13. Jerome, *Ep* 14.2.
14. *Ep* 413 is Bernard's letter to Abbot Rainald regarding this situation.

Bernard begins the letter unswervingly, stating the accusations against Alard: The novice Adamarus complained directly to Bernard that while the abbot was away Alard had treated him harshly, he had been driven from the abbey at Alard's direction, and then was not allowed back. Bernard tends to believe the novice since he knows Alard's tendency towards obstinacy. The abbot even reminds Alard of his own admission that he acknowledges this indomitable inclination. Bernard subtly accuses Alard of devious behavior for blaming someone else for the monk's expulsion.

Bernard states that he cares not why the novice was expelled, but rather the way in which the novice was treated. Despite Adamarus' humble satisfaction, his urgent prayers, his patience, and his promises of correction, Alard had not treated him with the love and reception required by the *Rule*.[15] Bernard demands that Alard receive him back mercifully so that "he does not withdraw from the just and merciful God." How Alard responds to Adamarus will influence the way Adamarus will respond to God. The health of the novice's soul is the primary issue at hand, and Alard's responsibility is to nurture this young man in the monastic faith, regardless of whatever personality conflicts Alard may have with him. Christian community must remain intact despite emotional conflicts that arise on occasion. For Bernard, the core issue in this situation was obedience. Both Adamarus and Alard had displayed disobedience in this matter. As a role model to Adamarus, Alard had the responsibility to demonstrate humility to the novice.

Bernard's involvement in this situation demonstrates the care to which he took his abbatial responsibilities. As a daughter house of Clairvaux, Foigny's events directly involved Bernard's attention. Alard's own ambitions combined with his lack of obedience to the *Rule* would directly affect the spiritual health of the entire monastic community. The letter clearly demonstrates that although Bernard's ecclesiastical activity kept him away from Clairvaux on many occasions, he was a director of souls who expected accountability to him.

LETTER 250 TO THE CARTHUSIAN PRIOR OF PORTES (1150)

The *Rule* uses the term 'prior' on many occasions, but does not specify any particular function other than serving as a superior in the monastery. In

---

15. *Rule*, 58.

the Cistercian tradition, the duty of the prior (or claustral prior) was to have charge of the monastery on the occasion that the abbot was away. In other times, the responsibilities and authority of the prior remained at the discretion of the abbot. In monasteries that had no abbot, a Conventual Prior assumed the abbatial role. In the twelfth-century, many Carthusian monasteries utilized a Conventual Prior.

Bernard wrote a handful of letters addressed to priors. It is unknown as to why he chose to write an abbey's prior rather than its abbot. Perhaps a different reason existed for each circumstance. However, with the abbot's reliance upon his own prior at Clairvaux, he must have seen the importance of choosing carefully the individual who would hold this essential position. *Letter 250*, written just three years before Bernard's death, is an interesting letter that contains perhaps the most often quoted sentences in the epistolary corpus. Absent from the epistle is a primary theme. Instead, the letter involves three separate issues. The first two regard the abbey of Portes and the second regards Bernard himself.

The monks of Portes felt frustration that one of their own was elected as a bishop, but then faced humiliation when Pope Eugenius III refused to confirm him. They took offense not only that Brother Noel was rejected by the Pope, but also that this situation has embarrassed their entire Order. They had received a previous letter from Bernard that somehow offended them, so the abbot begins this letter by attempting to clarify his earlier statements. He stresses that he has nothing but the utmost respect for their Order, even stating in a paraphrase of Psalm 68:10, "I am consumed with zeal for your house." He exhorts them not to be disheartened by the Pope's decision, but to understand why the Pope ruled as he did. The monks' defense of their Order is masking their real sin of ambition and pride. They appear to be more concerned with their Carthusian reputation than for trusting the wisdom of their spiritual father in Rome.

Bernard states that Brother Noel has some character flaws that even they knew existed. In fact, Bernard had observed these flaws before Noel's conversion. Another reason for his prohibition from becoming a bishop is that the Cistercian Pope did not want to confirm a new hermit like Noel. He needed more seasoning from the desert before he could be ready to become a bishop. Bernard writes that he knew nothing about this action. "You must know that I had not known of his decision, so no one can say that he did this at my instigation." Bernard encourages the prior to put this sad situation behind him, and to set his eyes on higher things.

The second issue Bernard addresses in this letter regards Bernard's displeasure upon hearing that an abbot had written a harsh letter to this Carthusian prior. He writes that when he has the opportunity, he will tell this abbot what he thinks about the letter. The prior of Portes should not allow this evil to overcome him, but rather to allow the strength of God to overcome this evil by good. In his own experience as a polarizing figure, Bernard knew quite well how to deal with critical people. He saw those opportunities as avenues for spiritual growth rather than a seedbed of growing resentment.

The final paragraph of this letter contains what is perhaps the most curious statement in the entire epistolary corpus. Bernard begins the paragraph by stating, "It is time not to forget myself." He asks the prior to pity his monstrous life and his afflicted conscience, and then proceeds with a self-evaluation of his life. "I am a kind of modern Chimæra," he writes, "neither cleric nor layman. Long ago I stripped myself from the monastic life, just not my habit." He states that he dare not restate what others have said about him or where they want to hurl him headfirst. Bernard is a tired, sickly man just a few years from death when he wrote these legendary words. Numerous scholars have exegeted these cryptic words and comment have offered theories regarding Bernard psychological and emotional states at the time. However, when understanding this interesting statement in the context of the letter, a clearer decipherment of this statement becomes known. This statement is more than self-examination, but a lesson in thankfulness.

The abbot had spent a majority of the letter consoling the Carthusian prior of Portes regarding the reputation of their abbey, their embarrassment, and the harshness with which they had been treated by the abbot of another monastery. The monks of the Portes abbey had been absorbed in their own reputation and standing in the church, and in the process had forgotten the plight of others. By making this "Chimæra" statement, Bernard is reminding the prior that they are not the only ones who had received criticism. His own life, sacrificed on behalf of the church, had become so monstrous and disfigured by the world that he was no longer able to live a Cistercian life. At least the monks of Portes, regardless of their reputation, could remain faithful to their conversion by remaining cloistered. Rather than focusing on the trials of their own existence, the monks of Portes should be thankful for the grace of God and forget their futile task of regaining their worldly reputation.

CONCLUSIONS

Bernard's letters to monks are ripe with examples of spiritual direction. Regardless of their abbey, he takes the role of their abbot, offering counsel that would not only affect their life on earth, but their soul in eternity. The importance of Bernard's letters to monks lies in his theological understanding of the importance of monastic faithfulness. For Bernard, a faithful monastic vocation was the surest means to heaven, although an unfaithful monk was in danger of the precipice of hell. When Bernard made the foundation of Clairvaux in 1115, the small Cistercian Order had been in existence for a mere twenty-five years. His belief in the Cistercian reformation ideal and its credibility in the church was the impetus for his correspondence with monks, even those outside of his own order. Throughout his letters to monks, recurring themes emerge.

First, Bernard stressed faithfulness to one's vocation as obedience to God. For the monk, this meant obedience to one's abbot, or in the case with the monk Adam of Morimond, obedience to the statutes of the Order. Obedience to oneself is the beginning of obedience to God. Bernard believed that this was the primary task of novices. Once a novice had conquered his own will, the peace of God could fill the vacuum. Monks who aspire only to be faithful monks, and not hold any other office in the church, were able to experience the joy and intimacy of Christ, serving their part in the overall faithfulness of his bride.

Second, faithfulness to Christ allows a monk to be faithful to his abbot. Faithfulness to his abbot allows a monk to be faithful to Christ. Faithfulness and obedience to Christ involves a synthesis between the personal and the ecclesiastical. A monk was not an individual, but a member of Christ's body, the church. The monk's humble service to Christ from behind the walls of the cloister was his participation in the mystical and incarnational nature of the church.

A final theme in Bernard's letters to monks is the vice of personal ambition. As persons who had abandoned the world to embrace Christ, monks had surrendered all personal aspirations. Although some in the church had attempted to mask ambition under the guise of serving Christ, monks should aspire only to what will draw them closer to Christ. Any other undertaking had dangerous spiritual consequences.

These themes are not exclusive unto themselves, but work together to define Bernard's ecclesiastical agenda. Although his methodology may be questioned, his purpose is quite clear. The spiritual counsel offered in his letters to monks were part of Bernard's greater agenda of seeing a church restored to the faithfulness of the apostles through the inner reformation of each person in the church. The abbot of Clairvaux believed he was the catalyst of his generation to see this come to fruition.

CHAPTER 5

The Letters of Bernard to Abbots

IN THE LETTERS TO abbots, Bernard was essentially writing to his peers. These abbots were his peers on record, but from the content and tone of these letters, one cannot imagine that many of these abbots who received letters from Bernard (particularly Cistercian abbots) understood themselves as equals in the mind of the authoritative abbot of Clairvaux. Through these letters, the abbot offered spiritual advice and counsel, expressed concern for their souls, conducted business, and articulated extreme disappointment in their actions. Although Bernard's emotional spontaneity sometimes flavored these letters, his desired outcome was the discipline and obedience of these abbatial leaders to be faithful to God. Bernard's expectations of them were high, but no higher than the expectations he had for himself. The abbot expected lofty standards from these abbots, for their faithfulness and obedience to the Rule would affect the spiritual lives of the men under their care. Similarly, since Bernard held that the health of the church in general depended upon the faithfulness of those in the monasteries, their abbatial faithfulness would provide a spiritual foundation for the entire church. Abbots were the spiritual fathers of their monks. As such, they had a paternalistic spiritual responsibility to them. An abbot who was unfaithful in his own obedience to Christ could hardly serve as a healthy spiritual model for his monks.

In the surviving corpus of Bernard's letters, 103 are addressed to abbots. Although Bernard could not have been a particularly good abbot due to his excessive travels and interests beyond the walls of Clairvaux, he nevertheless had much advice to offer his abbatial colleagues. The letters of Bernard to abbots range from outright criticism to unmitigated praise.

Where these letters find commonality is through the spiritual counsel Bernard offers in each of them. In his letters to abbots, Bernard addresses not only the importance of obedience, but also the idea that one's personal faithfulness to God affects the whole church. Bernard's desire to see the church return to the faithfulness of the apostles through the renewal of the monasteries is another prominent theme in his letters to abbots, for in Bernard's mind, renewal of the church would come through monastic expansion and abbatial leadership and obedience.

LETTERS OF ENCOURAGEMENT

Bernard knew the importance of extending credit to individuals when they deserved it; or more accurately, when a specific deed had pleased the abbot or had brought forth monastic renewal to their abbeys or orders. While Bernard praised abbots from time to time, he characterized the praise in one of three ways: (1) praise to God for their faithfulness, (2) praise to them for completing the work he himself had started in their lives, or (3) by praise to them for their perseverance in the midst of strife.

Letter 78 to Letter to Suger, Abbot of St. Denis (1127)

One of the most widely known letters to abbots is *Letter 78* to Suger, abbot of the Benedictine Abbey of St. Denis. A royal abbey, St. Denis had become not much more than a center for political meetings for the King of France and his entourage. The opulence with which the abbot of this supposed house of God would have lived would have made even the abbot of the great Cluny envious. Suger, named abbot of this important monastery by King Louis "*le gros*" in 1121–1122, was very comfortable dealing with the heads of state, and was apparently a wise choice by the King who needed an abbot with administrative skills and one who possessed etiquette appropriate for national and international dignitaries.

Suger, however, rather than tending to official business as usual, began to instigate spiritual reforms—returning the abbey to a place of prayer and solitude instead of a meetinghouse for the king. One wonders how well the French king knew Suger before appointing him as abbot, for these reforms would hardly serve the king's interests. In a letter worthy of being received by a powerful political leader like Suger, Bernard congratulated the abbot for having the courage to begin needed reforms and encouraged him to initiate even more changes.

Bernard begins by affirming not what Suger had done in his worldly past, but rather what God had done in Suger through his reforms of St. Denis. He writes, "Certainly all have heard of the good that God has made in your soul." Bernard makes it clear at the onset that it is God whom he is praising for what has occurred in Suger's life rather than the abbot himself. It was not the abbot of St. Denis who had instigated the reforms, but the Spirit of God working in and through Suger.

Following this introductory comment, Bernard makes use of surprisingly strong imageries of a violent military campaign. He compares the task of reforming a royal monastery to a military battle, a comment on the monumental task before Suger; and a reason that Bernard felt compelled to write such a lengthy letter supporting his abbatial colleague. In his attempts to bring about reforms to St. Denis, Bernard states that Suger has acted like a "vigorous soldier, or rather like a dutiful and strong officer." He writes that in this capacity as a ground officer, Suger runs back and forth along the soldiers' lines. With his bloody sword drawn and voice crying-out, he offers encouragement to the ailing troops as they battle against the enemy and are hewn down.

In Bernard's descriptive battle scene, he portrays Suger as a captain rallying his troops, symbolizing Bernard's belief that an abbot's responsibility was to engage in spiritual warfare for his monks. Not merely a passive observer who allowed monks to find their own way to God, an abbot, according to Bernard, is one who works side-by-side with his spiritual sons to ensure that they are kept safe from the flaming arrows of temptation.

In the section of the letter that follows, Bernard quickly apologizes for using a secular example to symbolize Suger's accomplishments when he could have used examples from scripture itself. The abbot then compares Suger to Moses, Jeremiah, the Apostle Paul, and King David. Since these spiritual leaders gave themselves completely to God's work, regardless of what it cost them personally, Suger must continue what he had started. Bernard reminds him that just as these biblical men faced personal opposition, Suger must remember that any murmurings in and around St. Denis were not directed to the entire community, but to the reforms of Suger directly. If Suger could not handle this negative attention, he should not instigate reforms. According to Bernard, reforming abbots need to take responsibility for their actions, and not be afraid to defend them, for their reforms were for the good of all.

Bernard then specifies to Suger which of the St. Denis reforms he believes to be the most significant. He states that in St. Denis he hears that God moves freely, discipline is carefully guarded, and spiritual reading is encouraged. Contrasting these new, positive reforms, Bernard compares the former life at St. Denis to the 'den of thieves' that Jesus called the Jerusalem temple that was conducting not spiritual, but temporal business (Matt 21:13). These reforms are to God examples of real *sacrificium laudem* (Ps 50:23) that Suger and his monks sing to God. For the St. Denis abbey to be used for anything but prayer is incomprehensible to Bernard. Monks have professed to remove themselves from the world. Due to its royal status, St. Denis has invited the world into its cloister. The King of France has asserted control over the monastery in the past. By enacting these reforms, Suger has reminded the king that God, and not he, reigns over the abbey. The King should know this, as church and state are called to work together in harmony, each respecting the other's domain.

However, rather than dwelling on praise for Suger, Bernard offers the abbot some wisdom on how to determine which type of human praise is worthy and which human praise is hypocritical. Bernard warns Suger to avoid those who spew *laudatur peccator*, or immoral praise, which intends to flatter the soul, but does not do so with love. True admiration is admiration grounded in the Lord, because that admiration acknowledges God. Bernard states that he praises Suger because he has deserved it. He certainly does not intend to flatter the reforming abbot. Bernard reminds Suger of the value of fearing vice no less than one cherishes virtues. Self-knowledge is a virtue that leads to humility, and humility keeps one from the vice of ambition. This counsel is designed affect Suger's own life, but Bernard's chief aim was Suger's affect on those around him, including the King of France.

LETTER 96 TO RICHARD, ABBOT OF FOUNTAINS (1133)

During the rapid growth of the Cistercian movement in the early twelfth century, much of this growth came from abbeys who desired to affiliate with a Cistercian monastery. The Fountains abbey in England was one of these monasteries that affiliated with Clairvaux in 1134–35. The foundation of the abbey began with a group of monks from St. Mary's Abbey in York, who became frustrated with its lax in monastic discipline. In 1132, they determined to leave and found a new monastery under Cistercian Rule. Bernard enthusiastically supported their endeavors. They encountered numerous hardships and threats, but were protected by their Archbishop, Thurstan. During the affiliation process, Bernard wrote to Richard, the abbot of Fountains, to congratulate him and his brothers on their decision to take the higher way by seeking a more rigorous monastic lifestyle.

In a style typical of the abbot when praising someone for making spiritual reforms, Bernard writes that he is thrilled how Richard is warming in the fresh fire of God. Richard, like Hezekiah, recovered from illness to health (Isa 38:9). Although he was weak, he is now filled with strength, blossoming like a flower into holiness. Bernard writes that prudence alone should have shown Richard that he should follow this better way, since mediocrity is so close to apostasy. In language reminiscent of Revelation 3:16, Bernard describes complacent monks as being *vomitum* from the mouth of God. A complacent monk is in a worse spiritual condition than a layperson, for monks have made a life-commitment to God of prayer and service, and thus should exhibit such a life. Since a layperson has not made such a vow, he or she cannot be judged on the same level of mediocrity. The monastic community is an example to the church of faithfulness to Christ. When one within that community fails to demonstrate this Christlikeness, that monk's life is no different than the taste of vomit (in contrast to the taste of sweetness) in the mouth of God.

It is not difficult to discern how Richard might have reacted to this letter. He had begun reforms in his abbey, and was in the process of affiliating with Clairvaux. If he failed to complete this task, he knew very well what Bernard's opinion would be of him. This letter is one of praise for Richard's reforms, but it also contains a subtle reminder to continue them. This suggestion to Richard is a reminder that affiliating with Clairvaux entails strict accountability and carefully measured reforms. It also may serve as an inherent reminder that Bernard himself will be watching for Abbot Richard's promised reforms. Bernard's understanding of Christian accountability included the consummation of one's promises and intentions.

Letter 254 to Warren, Abbot of the Alps (1136)

Warren became the abbot of Our Lady of the Alps in Switzerland in 1113. When Bernard wrote this letter to Warren in 1136, Warren was sixty-one years old. Two years later, the abbey was incorporated into the Cistercian order. Regarding the process of abbeys affiliating with the Cistercian Order, Bernard always stressed the purity of the Rule as a function of the purity of heart, in function of the vision of God. In a very formal letter to Warren, Bernard praises the future saint for his virtuous life. This letter, filled with rich counsel and praise, is written as though Bernard had deep respect and admiration for his elder abbot, yet written as though Bernard himself is the one with the authority over an elder. His tone is respectful, yet from the perspective of a young abbot who does not view himself as less experienced than the veteran Warren, who had been abbot for twenty-three years.

Bernard writes that Warren's body is growing cold with age, but his heart is glowing with warmth. He praises Warren for not becoming weary or burdened with his age by allowing his spirit to continue growing strong as his body becomes weak. Bernard clearly has admiration for Warren, and the letter reads as if Bernard hopes that one day he himself will face death with the same glowing heart and peaceful spirit. The faithfulness of Warren moves Bernard's heart, but he cannot resist encouraging the aging abbot to continue striving toward holiness, even in his old age. He comments (perhaps even self-referentially) that vigorous souls do not always lie in strong and energetic bodies, for sometimes they are in weak and sickly bodies. Bernard praises Warren for his restoration of the vigor of his community, and that his godly life has served as a living example to all his spiritual sons. As the abbot of Clairvaux did not know the state of Warren's health, he took advantage of the opportunity to share this spiritual encouragement with him. In fact, Warren's death was not imminent, for four years later he would be elected Bishop of Sion in Switzerland.

LETTERS OF DISAPPOINTMENT

As Bernard's expectations for abbots were high, it is no surprise that on occasion he would find their actions either disappointing or at times deplorable. Since their abbatial task involved the direction of souls, their own lives and vocational commitment must be grounded in Christ. However, as several of these letters demonstrate (particularly the ones written to abbots of his own order), Cistercian abbots were not always the pious, holy men they aspired to be. As public leaders in the Cistercian movement, they represented to others the monastic reform Bernard strived to see realized throughout the church. These abbots were humans who made errors in judgment. Yet, they also knew the reality that they were unofficially accountable to Bernard when they made these decisions of indiscretion.

LETTER 4 TO ARNOLD, ABBOT OF MORIMOND (1124)

Perhaps the best known of these letters is *Letter 4*, written to Arnold, abbot of Morimond, who left his abbey with a handful of monks for a pilgrimage to Jerusalem. Arnold and Bernard had been in Citeaux together, so the abbot probably knew him and his *obstionationem* well.[1]

Bernard's emotional appeal to Arnold to return to his abbey is based primarily not on the abbot's obligations to the Cistercian order, but on Arnold's responsibility as a spiritual father to his monks. Bernard does, however, twice include the line *O magna nostri ordinis columna!* ("O great foundation of our Order!") Although Bernard argues that Arnold's disobedience could result in the collapse of the entire order itself, he remains firm in his assertion that Arnold's primary mistake was leaving his spiritual sons without a father. Certainly, Bernard had the public reputation of the young Cistercian order in mind as he dealt with this situation and composed the letter, but as an abbot himself, Bernard knew that in many ways, the monks' souls depended upon their abbot. Arnold was placed in a position of authority not for his own sake, but for the sake of others; not to promote his own interests, but the interests of Christ. Leaving his flock was a selfish act, unbecoming of one who has been called to keep away the spiritual wolves of the world. Bernard reminds him of the foundations that Morimond has made in recent years, and asks him what will happen to those abbeys who need his spiritual leadership, as well.

Appealing to Arnold's sense of reason, he asks the wayward abbot to judge what good could possibly come from this situation; or if no good, then what evils could result from it. Bernard's lack of situational compromise in dealing with Arnold demonstrates the abbot's tendency to characterize situations (and to some extent individuals) as either good or evil. Centrism was certainly not part of Bernard's ideological framework! In this instance, absolutely no good could come from Arnold's decision to leave his abbey. For him to embark upon this journey without the counsel of any

---

1. Since Bernard also displayed a tendency for stubbornness, this may have given him a keener insight into Arnold's decision to leave his duty. An account of the General Chapter's discussion of this matter can be found in Canivez, *Statuta capitulorum generalium ordinis Cisterciensis*, 1:4–5.

of his brother abbots demonstrates a pride of heart, since Arnold surely would have known what their counsel would have been. Arnold's monks willingly submitted to his spiritual leadership in leaving for Jerusalem. However, Arnold's submission was to no one, including his own will.

Ironically, later in his own life, Bernard would embark on his own journeys across Christendom to settle disputes and engage himself in the controversial affairs of the world; leaving the spiritual lives of his monks in the hands of others. However, Bernard would argue that what separated his many expeditions from Arnold's single trip is that Bernard's journeys were not motivated by selfishness. Arnold left his abbey for his own desires, while Bernard always maintained that he was drawn away from Clairvaux by the needs of the church.

LETTER 397 TO ODO, ABBOT OF MARMOUTIER (1124–1137)

Another example of Bernard's disappointment with an abbot is found in Letter 397, an epistle sent to Odo, Abbot of Marmoutier, sent under the names of Bernard and Hugh of Pontigny. By sending this letter to Odo from both himself and Hugh, Bernard wanted the abbot of Marmoutier to understand that the situation had to do with more than just the opinion of one Cistercian abbot. The situation in which Odo had placed himself was a reflection upon the entire Order.

The two abbots are concerned about a rumor about Odo and his abbey. Odo has had a reputation of sanctity that is being tarnished: the rumor is that Odo and his monks have become more concerned with receiving revenues owed to them than on maintaining a life of simplicity and holiness. Bernard writes, "It is not right, brothers, not right that you should esteem temporal profit over your witness." In other words, Odo should be willing to give up rights to revenue in order to save his and his abbey's reputation, which are worth far more than any financial gain. Bernard counsels Odo that for a monk, it is better to possess a little and live in peace than to possess a lot and live in dispute. Is the amount Odo and his abbey would gain in this quarrel over revenue worth the sacrifice of inner peace and sanctity? The actions Abbot Odo takes regarding its business affairs will affect the entire abbey, not only financially, but spiritually. In essence, Bernard exhorts Odo to reconsider the spiritual dimensions of his role as abbey administrator.

The financial pressures on these medieval abbots must have been tremendous, for as the monastic movement gained momentum, competition for revenue became increasingly intense as abbots vied for benefactors and land for expansion. As a medieval abbot, Bernard understood this. However, since Clairvaux had become famous due to its revered abbot (and had become the darling of many beneficiaries) he may not have actually experienced these financial struggles for several years. As part of society, monasteries had temptations for power and growth, but Bernard's desire is that they would never forget their first calling of seeking holiness by fleeing the world. By living a life of prayer and sanctity, abbots are more disposed to approach administration and political dealings with a greater awareness of God's presence and security.

LETTERS OF VOCATIONAL EXHORTATION

Nearly every letter written by the abbot of Clairvaux can be considered examples of spiritual exhortation. The abbot had an abundance of advice to share with individuals in nearly every strata of society. However, several letters, by the very nature of their content and purpose, exemplify this genre more particularly than others. These letters, some often quite amusing, offer a glimpse into the daily lives of medieval abbots. Surely, these men of God must have felt enormous pressure to ensure the spiritual lives of their monks and to preserve the financial needs of their abbey. Bernard offered an abundance of spiritual exhortations to his fellow abbots, covering both their individual spirituality and general vocational issues.

THE RAINALD LETTERS

The abbey of Foigny was founded from Clairvaux in 1121. For its first abbot Bernard chose Rainald, a monk of Clairvaux and presumably a man of character. In a series of letters written over the span of a several years, Bernard and Rainald corresponded with each other frequently. Although Rainald's activities as abbot were in order, Bernard finds himself becoming increasingly frustrated with him. The letters that survive are fine examples of Bernard's style of writing to someone he knows well, and to someone with whom he has high expectations.

In *Letter 72* (1121–1122), Bernard responds to a letter from Rainald, in which the abbot of Foigny extols the praises of the future saint. Rainald missed Clairvaux desperately, and Bernard writes to encourage him to focus more on his duty as an abbot than on showering Bernard with praises and titles. Bernard is concerned that Rainald is focusing so intently on Bernard and his memories of Clairvaux that he cannot possibly provide the spiritual attention and care necessary for his monks. In addition, Rainald is focusing his praise and support upon Bernard, and not God, which Bernard declares to be dangerous ground. In the spirit of 2 Corinthians 1:23, Bernard writes that in Rainald's best interest Bernard should not dominate over him, but rather rejoice with him in all that God would do through him as abbot of Foigny. The relationship between Bernard and Rainald has changed from that of father/brother to that of brother/brother. Rainald must accept this in order to serve effectively as an abbot. Rainald is himself a spiritual father, and as such he must accept the responsibility placed upon him.

While Rainald may have the ability to lead a monastery, lacking in him is the spiritual maturity necessary to accept his new role. God has placed him in this position of leadership through the monastic election process. Rainald's hesitation in assuming this new role and longing for the simplicity of his former life is nothing more than pride. From Bernard's perspective, Rainald's actions represent ambition, for he selfishly longs for a monastic vocation that he desires, not the one that God desires for him. Fulfilling the role of an abbot requires the spiritual ability and personal willingness to serve as an incarnational presence in the lives of monks. They must exhibit the characteristics of Christ, led by prayer, and empowered by the Holy Spirit. This demands selflessness, even when one does feel adequate for the position.

In *Letter 73* (1122–1123) the second letter in this series, Bernard writes to a Rainald who is anxious, bewildered, and sorrowful in his role as abbot. From the context of this letter, it seems clear that Rainald wrote to Bernard with a long list of complaints about being an abbot. He wanted to return to the cloister of Clairvaux and leave the burden of the abbacy behind him. Rainald did not like dealing with the many needs of monks, who had become more of a burden to him than a comfort. Bernard shows little patience with Rainald and challenges him to stop focusing on his own situation and to deal with the spiritual lives of his monks. Bernard writes that in the acts of comforting, encouraging, and reproving, Rainald would be doing his duty by carrying the burdens of others; and in the process, bringing healing to them. Focusing on his own needs is not the duty of an abbot; abbots are called to focus on directing the souls of their spiritual sons. Just as Christ came to serve others and not himself, Rainald must be Christ to those in Foigny. Since Rainald's life is not following the selfless example of Christ, Bernard has concerns for the new abbot's spiritual well being. Jesus, the pinnacle of selfless living, demonstrated self-sacrifice to his disciples. His example has provided a pattern for all Christians to follow. Rainald's ambitious selfishness must cease, for in his actions he is not modeling Christ to his monks, but selfish ambition.

However, Bernard did not desire for Rainald to think he cared little for him and closes the letter with an encouraging word. Bernard writes that he is sending the prior of Clairvaux to Foigy, whose words will be much more comforting to Rainald than Bernard's written text. Bernard certainly does not want to ignore Rainald's spiritual and emotional needs, and by sending the prior to visit him, Bernard hopes this will demonstrate his continued love and support for Rainald. In conclusion, Bernard writes that he hopes Rainald knows that the two of them are of the same mind and will. Hyperbole or not, this statement offers encouragement to Rainald. Bernard knows that harsh aspersion would not foster confidence in this fragile abbot. This statement reminds Rainald of the new brother-brother relationship shared by these two Cistercians. While not explicitly addressing the issue at hand, Bernard insinuates the situation of Rainald's desire to please Bernard. They are peers focused on pleasing Christ through by directing the souls of the monks under their care.

In the final letter to Rainald, *Letter 74* (1125–1131), Bernard seems exceptionally frustrated. He writes that in his last letter, Bernard chided him for constantly worrying him with his many problems and anxieties. It seems that Rainald took his former abbot's advice too well and stopped corresponding with Bernard completely. In not hearing from Rainald in several months, Bernard became more anxious for him than ever before. In a curious reversal from *Letter 72*, in which Bernard instructs Rainald to see himself not as Bernard's son, but brother, in this instance Bernard refers to Bernard as his *filius*, and instructs Rainald no longer to hide anything that is happening to him. Bernard had lost trust in Rainald to handle his abbatial affairs independently, and so was now assuming close, direct supervision over him once again. In a final (and somewhat comical) statement of authority over Rainald, Bernard concludes the letter by asking the troubled abbot to return the books he borrowed.

These three letters offer tremendous insight into Bernard's spiritual leadership style. In this instance, Bernard placed someone in a position of leadership, watched him grow into the position, corrected him in hope of increasing his leadership potential, and then realized his leadership limitations and taking control of supervising him more closely. Bernard demonstrates tremendous patience in this situation with Rainald. Rather than removing the troubled abbot from his duties and returning him to Clairvaux, Bernard kept him in the position for his own spiritual growth. Bernard understood that returning Rainald to Clairvaux would not serve as the best solution, even if it resulted in a more effective abbot at Foigny. This meant a greater burden on him personally, but Bernard seemed willing to take on this responsibility for Rainald's own well-being (and perhaps the overall health of the Foigny abbey).

However, this situation with Rainald might be perceived in a different way. While Bernard stated that he expected Rainald to understand himself as Bernard's peer, it seems that when Rainald did as his former abbot exhorted him to do, Bernard became displeased. Although Bernard wrote that he desired Rainald to assume a peer-relationship with him, it served only to ensure success in Rainald's abbacy. Bernard may not have wanted to relinquish control over Rainald at all. This third letter seems quite clear that the abbot of Clairvaux felt the need to be overly involved in the lives of others (or in modern terminology, Bernard could be seen as a micromanager). He appears not to trust others' capacity for responsible spiritual self-care.

LETTERS REGARDING REFORM IN YORK

When the Cistercians arrived in England in 1132 with the establishment of the abbey of Rievaulx, the Benedictine monasteries felt the effects. Within these Benedictine abbeys were monks who desired a stricter way of life, and they began to put pressure on their abbots. The first abbey to experience this tension was St. Mary's abbey in York. As mentioned above, in October of 1132, two monks, the prior and sub-prior, together with their followers, began a plot to bring about reforms they believed were necessary for the spiritual vitality of the community. Abbot Geoffrey was old, tired, and not willing to put the community through stresses of enacting reforms. The prior, Richard, sought help from Thurstan, Archbishop of York. When Thurstan arrived at the abbey to provide counsel, Geoffrey refused him admission. Threatened with violence by their own St. Mary's brethren, Richard and his reforming monks left for the safety of Thurstan's home. A few months later Thurstan installed Richard and his companions on uncultivated land, since the Cistercian ideal included a foundation in the solitude of the wilderness. This foundation would become the abbey of Fountains.[2]

Abbot Geoffrey, wanting to find a peaceful compromise to this situation and the return of his monks, wrote Bernard of Clairvaux for counsel. However, the response he received may not have been what he was expecting. Bernard begins *Letter 94* (1133) as if Geoffrey was bothering him: "You write me from across the sea to seek my counsel, but I wish you had looked somewhere else." Bernard writes that regarding the monks who had left Geoffrey, he believes it was of God, because they have remained resolute in their purpose. Bernard was not going to encourage monks with a reforming ideal to abandon that ideal for any purpose, and certainly not to return to an abbot who refused reform. Monastic obedience was to Christ, particularly when a non-reforming superior was involved.

While the role of obedience as a means of faithfulness to Christ is a recurring theme in Bernard's letters, Bernard's understanding of monastic obedience was not always consistent with the *Rule*, particularly with regard to himself. Bernard understands obedience to mean submission to one's superior only when that individual is living a life of faithfulness to Christ. Of course, the situational subjectivity of this logic seems problematic, but for Bernard, the logic was quite clear.

Bernard quotes Gregory the Great to the aging Geoffrey as a way of bringing authority to his argument. Quoting from Gregory's *Pastoral Rule* and his commentary on Ezekiel, Bernard argues that it is sinful for anyone who has sought a more holy life to abandon it for a former way of life. Geoffrey should abandon his attempts to retrieve his monks because it would not be well for his own soul to extinguish their spirit. Geoffrey should take pride in the fact that his sons have a desire for progress in the spiritual life. They have moved in a direction they believe God has called them by first examining their inner motivations and subsequently seeking a more ascetic monastic lifestyle.

In a second letter, *Letter 313* (1133) written again in response to correspondence from Geoffrey, Bernard explains in more detail why Geoffrey should let his monks go. Although Geoffrey has called his monks *apostatae* for disobeying him and abandoning their monastery, Bernard will not condemn them. He suggests that by his actions, Geoffrey is placing the small things before the great (*praeponderant minora maioribus*). Although the

---

2. Knowles, *The Monastic Order in England*, 231–39.

explicit counsel here is that Geoffrey is focusing on retrieving his monks instead of focusing on their own spiritual progress, a precise spiritual lesson to Geoffrey is also involved here. The abbot of St. Mary is placing his own minor egotistical needs before the greater spiritual needs of his sons. This de-emphasis on the temporal in favor of the eternal is the reason why Geoffrey is so distraught. Although this letter is written by a frustrated Bernard, he offers his brother abbot a spiritual lesson in pride in the midst of this political turmoil.

LETTER 69 TO GUY, ABBOT OF TROIS-FONTAINES

Several of Bernard's letters to abbots deal specifically (and quite interestingly) with abbots who turned to him with questions regarding specific incidents in their monasteries. These replies from Bernard provide details into the everyday details of twelfth-century monastic life, and of the many pressures these medieval abbots faced on a daily basis. These letters addressing practical matters demonstrate Bernard's care for the ordinary activities of his fellow abbots, and how even the most seemingly insignificant events can have great implications.

Trois-fontaines abbey was founded by Clairvaux in 1119. Bernard, not shying from using his family's influence, involved both a cousin and a maternal uncle in securing the site and physical foundation of the new abbey. In *Letter 69*, Bernard replies their abbot, Guy, who in horror discovered during Mass that the chalice server filled the cup not with wine, but water. Making a quick decision, he decided to continue the liturgy without the wine. Since the blood of Christ was absent, Guy wrote to Bernard to ask what should be done to remedy the situation. Bernard handles this situation with calm counsel, sympathizing with Guy. He knows that Guy is upset, and attempts to console him, yet without freeing him from the burden of the mistake. He tells Guy that on an occasion such as this, to be too angry with oneself is as much a sin as not being angry at all. Bernard's council to Guy is that taking responsibility for one's actions is necessary, but overdoing the self-anger is a focus on the self, or pride. Since this situation could serve as a spiritual lesson to Guy's monks, the abbot's actions following the mistake are critical.

Bernard prescribes a penance both to Guy and to the one who served the Mass that stipulated they are to recite the penitential Psalms and seven prostrations every day until Easter. For the incompetent chalice preparer,

Bernard leaves his penance to Guy's discretion. If any other monk heard of this error, they are to recite the penitential Psalms once, as a means of sharing one another's burdens. Bernard shares with Guy that under the circumstances, the abbot did the best he could do, and Bernard does not fault him for making the most of a difficult situation. Bernard then places himself in Guy's position and ponders how he would have handled the situation himself. Bernard deduces that if he found himself in the abbot's situation, he probably would have presented the wine at a later time, for the delay would not have nullified the consecration of the bread.

By empathizing with Guy, Bernard demonstrates his ability to get outside of himself and to envision a situation from a different perspective. Instead of simply telling Guy what he should have done, Bernard admits not knowing precisely the direct course he would have taken, but rather writes in the form of a running narrative in his mind.

This letter is intriguing on several levels. First, it serves as an example of a specific priestly error regarding the sacraments. Having no Host during mass was a grave offense, as for some, the Sacred Host was as holy as a relic. If the Sacred Host was absent in the Mass, the forgiveness of sins could not be granted. Bernard understood that Christ's presence did not reside exclusively in the Eucharistic elements. Therefore, Christ was still present during the mass. However, the fact that Guy had foolishly allowed this to happen was a severe negligence in the direction of his monks' souls, for it demonstrated to his monks that their abbot did not take seriously his priestly responsibilities.

A second significant aspect of this letter is that Bernard does not simply dismiss the error, but places it in perspective and then orders a rather light penance. The abbot of Clairvaux acknowledges that since several interpretations of the presence of Christ during mass exist, Guy's penance cannot be too severe. In fact, Bernard sees no scandal in these multiple interpretations of Christ's presence, stating that in this matter one must believe in a way that seems best to the individual. This statement by Bernard is intriguing, for he seems to be advocating a pluralistic theology of the Eucharist.

This letter demonstrates Bernard's approach to penance and forgiveness as a means of spiritual direction. In Sermon 40 of *Sermones de diversis*, Bernard outlines seven steps of penance: knowledge of oneself, repentence, sorrow, oral confession, mortification of the flesh, correction by a work, and perseverance.[3] This sacramental process was meant to reconcile an individual with God, not serve as a punitive route to forgiveness. For Bernard, penance is a means of experiencing God's grace, for through the physical hardships of penance people are able to "soothe their irritated conscience."[4] This process happens in the Christian community. As a director of Guy's soul, Bernard accepted his role in assigning penance. However, Guy has responsibility to the chalice bearer, so the assigning of penance is his responsibility for the monk's formation in Christ.

Through this letter, Bernard exhibits an ability to guide an individual who is truly disheartened and who desires to make amends through a process of forgiveness, restoration, and the attainment of hope. Bernard understood the genuineness of Guy's heart and took the time to present a systematic approach to remedy the problem. *Letter 69* helps to establish the argument that Bernard's spiritual counsel was situational. Rather than employing a standard course of counsel, Bernard based his spiritual exhortations on his knowledge of individuals. The counsel Bernard exhibits in letter reflects his trust of Guy's character. Guy had no ambitious agenda, but a heart for obedience. This is demonstrated by the fact that Guy was so distraught about the implications of this error that he risked his very abbatial position by informing Bernard of the mistake. From Guy's perspective, his abbatial error could affect his own salvation. Bernard's response is to comfort his friend without downplaying the grievous nature of the event. However, Bernard places most of the blame for the missing Host not on Guy, but on the chalice server, to whom Bernard allows Guy to assign penance.

Letter 79 to Luke, Abbot of Cuissy (1135–1148)

In *Letter 79* to Luke, Abbot of the Premonstratensian abbey of Cuissy, Bernard responds to the abbot's request for counsel regarding a difficult situation with one of his monks and a woman who worked with the lay brothers. Evidently, this brother was either found to be in an intimate relationship with the woman or else he confessed to the sin. Luke sought Bernard's guidance in how to handle the situation, indicating the approachability of Bernard by those in need of counsel, including those outside of the Cistercian Order.

3. *Div* 40; *SBOp* 6/1:234–42.
4. *Conv* 38; *SBOp* 4:114.

In a classic Bernard style, he puts forth the question of why Luke came to him in the first place. He writes that Luke should have gone to others more close to Cuissy, such as William of St. Thierry or even men of his own Premonstratensian order. However, since Luke came to Bernard, he cannot resist offering counsel. Bernard reasons that since the sin entailed people outside the abbey, Luke should handle the situation differently than if it happened inside the walls of the cloister. He encourages Luke to send the erring brother to a more remote Premonstratensian house (rather than a Cistercian monastery) in order to do penance. Bernard concludes his letter with some needed advice on abbatial decision-making. He refers to the abbey's mill where lay brothers encounter women on a regular basis. This is a dangerous situation, and one in which Luke has three options: he can forbid all women to enter the mill, he can put the mill in charge of secular people, or he can abandon the mill completely.

Taking for granted the monks' spiritual ideals and not realizing the danger of placing young celibate men in the company of women is a sign that the abbot of Cuissy does not understand his sons. Although Bernard comes close to stating this, in an uncharacteristic approach he allows Luke the opportunity to come to this conclusion himself. Bernard knows that forcing Luke to reason this on his own will make him a better abbot, both in relation to his monks and in his relations with those outside his abbey. Luke's naïveté is damaging in two ways: it hinders him from a successful abbacy, and it is an obstacle for the spiritual growth of his monks. The counsel Bernard offers Luke stresses the synthesis between one's vocational and personal identities. He knows Luke must decide what is best for his abbey, but as the spiritual father of his monastery, Luke must make this decision for himself.

LETTERS REGARDING MONKS

Just as the life of a good father revolves around the care and maturity of his children, the life of an abbot centers on the spiritual direction of his monks. When Bernard wrote to abbots, invariably the content of the letters included issues with one or more monks. Although nearly every abbatial letter mentions these spiritual sons, Bernard wrote several of them specifically regarding monks, either those who were wayward, those who desired to transfer to a Cistercian house, or clashes between them. For an abbot whose world was focused on far more than just the affairs of his own abbey

and the spiritual welfare of his own monks, Bernard always had counsel
for how his colleagues should handle certain situations. The spiritual guidance Bernard offers in these letters is demonstrative of the type of direction
Bernard desires the abbots to offer their monks.

Letter 76 to the Abbot of the Canons of St. Pierremont

The abbot of the Canons of St. Pierremont had a dilemma. It seems that a
married man became a monk with the blessing of his wife. While he was
in St. Pierremont, his wife died. Subsequently, the man decided that the
monastic way of life was not for him and left his vocation. He soon married a second wife. The abbot was concerned about the soul of the man
as well as the appearance of scandal. Bernard's counsel is straightforward:
the man should find a legal way to leave his wife and return to the abbey
immediately.

Bernard's concern is not the man's wife, nor his marriage. The dual
issues involved are the man's call to the monastic vocation and the church
as the Bride of Christ. Bernard begins his argument not with the man's marriage, but with his initial commitment to God. Bernard writes that for the
man, the situation is both unsafe and potentially unlawful for him to return
to the secular world after wearing a religious habit. Bernard is concerned
for the man's eternal soul, not for his temporal marriage. An individual's
vocational call from God takes precedence over everything else. Bernard
goes on not to blame the man exclusively for this situation, but he places
responsibility on the abbot himself. In no small part, the situation was his
fault. The abbot should have not deferred the man's readmission, which
gave the devil the chance to trap him into marriage. Now the abbot should
set things right by making sure they are separated in marriage, either by
the woman's own free will or through the intervention of the bishop. This
occasion affords Bernard the opportunity to explore the issues of Christian
marriage in relation to the church as the Bride of Christ.

The premise of love between the Bride and the Bridegroom dominates
Bernard's ecclesiology. Their mutual, intimate love binds them together in-
separably. Although Bernard describes the corporate church as the Bride,
he also understands the Bride as having an individual component, as well.
Bernard defines the Bride corporally in Sermon 68 of the *Song of Songs* but
qualifies the relationship as not being equal by any means. The fact that the
Bridegroom loves the lowly, earthly Bride demonstrates the intimate love

he has for her.[5] The Incarnation was a selfless demonstration of love by Christ, who placed the welfare of the Bride above his own. On earth, Christ has empowered humanity to represent the godhead in God's Kingdom, with God's people living selflessly as Christ demonstrated on earth.

Although he refers to the image of the Bride as the corporate church, he refers to the individual as the 'friend' of the Bridegroom. In *Letter 111* to Thomas, Provost of Beverly, the abbot writes to encourage young Thomas to fulfill his promise to enter Clairvaux, contrasting a friend of the world with a friend of the Bridegroom. Whereas a friend of the world is distracted by the tempting calls of the world, the friend of the Bridegroom "stands and rejoices with delight because of the Bridegroom's voice." Friends of Christ are not distracted by the world, but wait in anticipation for him. Likewise, Christ demonstrates his love by his very act of disposing himself to humanity.[6] The mystery of Christ's union with both the individual and the church makes his love multidimensional. Because Christ became human, Bernard maintains that love for Christ begins with a fleshly love and extends to a mysterious, mystical love.[7] The ability of Christ's love to influence both the body and the spirit makes his love a complete love, which is unlike any other love humans can experience. The friends of the Bridegroom, he writes, have received the Spirit of God, who has infused within them both virtues and gifts.[8] Bernard likens a friend of the Bridegroom to the person who "keeps watch over himself. . .that at the Bridegroom's arrival the lamp of his conscience will not empty of fuel and become extinguished."[9] Friends of the Bridegroom are the faithful representatives of the Bridegroom and thus must protect his reputation and ideals. Regarding the former monk of this letter, in order to remain a chaste member of the Bride of Christ, he must return to his first love, for marriage to Christ takes precedence over marriage to a human.

---

5. Michael Casey suggests that in Bernard the very act of the Word of God becoming human demonstrates Christ's desire to enter into a relationship of wedlock with the human race. *Athirst for God*, 194.

6. *SC* 68.2; *SBOp* 1:197.

7. McGinn, *The Growth of Mysticism*, 174.

8. See *SC* 70.8; *SBOp* 1:212.

9. *Ep* 42; *SBOp* 7:116.

LETTER 102 TO A CERTAIN ABBOT (BEFORE 1151)

In *Letter 102*, Bernard writes to an abbot who was having difficulties with a difficult monk (*fratre turbato, et turbante fratres*). This monk seemed unredeemable, and the abbot desired counsel from Bernard on how to deal with him. Bernard's response is straight from chapter 28 of Benedict's *Rule* regarding brothers who do not respond to correction from their abbots and from the words of the apostle Paul in 1 Corinthians 5:13: "Put away the evil one, for it is better for one to be put away so the rest will not be led into evil." His language becomes more severe, as he compares the evil monk to a diseased sheep or a gangrenous limb that needs to be amputated. He admonishes the abbot not to see this view as a lack of love, for the real love is how he will free the entire body from this evil part.

The overall spiritual health of the abbey is Bernard's concern, and he encourages the abbot to take this same view. The whole is greater than the individual. It is better that one should perish than that the unity of all should suffer. This is strong language, yet Bernard needs to make a point. The faithful monks in his care need his attention and love. Dealing with the problem monk immediately will ensure that the abbot's focus can return to the other monks. The abbot should take this advice, for these ideas, after all, do not originate with Bernard, but with Benedict. Arguably, Bernard's understanding of unity originated with the Cistercian understanding of *unitas*. With the unity of the Trinity as our model, members of Christ's church must so live that nothing on earth can divide them. Although the union of the Trinity is an aspect of God's divine nature, *unitas spiritus* is achieved on earth through corporate unity in the Body of Christ.

This letter clearly demonstrates how the genius of Bernard appears in the very midst of his human challenges. Bernard was not an angelic presence in the church. He did not live a spotless life. Perhaps what made Bernard a successful spiritual director is his vulnerability to appear less-than-stoic at times. The earthiness of his personality gave him sincerity. He had a clear understanding of the human condition, and used this perception to persuade the opinions of others through exhortation and counsel.

LETTERS REGARDING MONASTIC REFORM

Letters regarding monks have reforming principles woven throughout them, as do Bernard's letters of disappointment, in which he maintained standards that encouraged abbatial reform. A few letters, however, are clearly concentrated on monastic reform. Bernard wrote them to encourage the recipients to maintain their spiritual zeal, and to offer advice on how to implement the reforms he believed were essential for the church.

LETTER 83 TO SIMON, ABBOT OF ST. NICOLAS (1121–1122)

St. Nicolas was a Clunaic monastery. In Simon's attempt to implement reforms, his monks rebelled. Simon needed support, and who better to offer counsel than a reformer? Bernard had been abbot of Clairvaux for no more than six or seven years when Simon wrote this letter, but Bernard's reputation had already spread throughout the region. Written four years before the publication of his *Apologia*, this letter serves as an example of a young reformer who was already beginning to encourage non-Cistercian abbots who desired to introduce reforms.

In this early letter of Bernard, he offers consolation and advice to this well-meaning abbot of St. Nicolas. Bernard begins the letter by stating, "The persecutions you are suffering for justice moved me to compassion when I read your letter." Bernard understood the unswerving commitment needed by leaders to instigate reforms, which enabled him to empathize with Simon. Quoting 1 Timothy 3:12, Bernard reminds Simon that all who desire to live faithfully for Christ Jesus will suffer persecution. He counsels Simon to ease the severity of his reforms, so as not to ignore the salvation of the weak. The wisdom of this spiritual counsel resides in Bernard's understanding that reform can occur only through willing participants. As some are more willing for reform than others are, tempering one's zeal is not defeat. Rather, it is contextualizing one's situation that ensures that reform is enacted.

Bernard's language then turns to the same rhetorical style that he would use years later in one of his sermons on the Song of Songs in which he refers to dealing with heretics, *fides suadenda est, non imponenda* ("faith should be persuaded, not forced").[10] He says that when it comes to reforming the Cluniacs, they should be invited and not forced to a stricter way of life. The message Bernard is trying to convey is that while it is possible to force an individual's actions, one cannot force another's will. Persuasion leading to individual commitment is the means to individual—and then corporate—reform.

10. *SC* 66; *SBOp* 2:187.

A major aspect of Bernard's anthropology is that of human freedom. He defines freedom as the ability to consent voluntarily, which he understands to be a self-determining habit of the soul that separates us from the animals.[11] Human freedom of choice is so important to Bernard that he can state, "Take away free choice and there is nothing to be saved. Take away grace and there is no means of saving."[12] For Bernard, free choice is a necessary aspect of Christ's redeeming work in the soul, making it a center of a person's being.[13]

Because God has entrusted humanity with the capacity to make choices freely, Bernard placed great responsibility on the stewardship of free will. In the Fall, Adam did not cherish the free choice inherent in his being, and he misused it, to the detriment of all who followed him. Throughout his letters, Bernard takes quite seriously the decisions of others, contemplating why they could have been so careless, so naïve, or so noncommittal in the execution of their decisions. In fact, nearly every letter expects that the recipient will make a freely chosen decision that will have lasting influence in either his or her own life or in the life of the church. Bernard's scathing letter to his cousin Robert, who left Clairvaux for Cluny, is one such example. Another example is *Letter 247* to Pope Eugenius, in which Bernard questions the audacity of the pope for removing the pallium from an archbishop Bernard respected. He chastises the pope for not taking more care in making the decision. While at times Bernard finds it difficult explicitly not to tell people what decision to make, he offers counsel (some might call it manipulation) that might help them make a decision. For the abbot of Clairvaux, having a free will comes with responsibility.

In Bernard's first Parable, the story of the king and his son, the saint describes the king as Almighty God who created humanity with free will so that his choice of good should be voluntary instead of compelled.[14] God has endowed humanity with the capacity to make choices freely so that humanity might experience the joy of making the choice of good over evil. Love is never coerced but is always freely expressed and given. Of course, the ability to choose good over evil allows the possibility of choosing evil over good, which is the premise of Bernard's first parable, in which a son

---

11. Because animals do not have the ability to reason, Bernard maintains they do not have the ability to make free choices. *Gra* 15; *SBOp* 3:177.

12. *Gra* 2; *SBOp* 3:166.

13. McGinn, *Growth of Mysticism*, 169.

14. *Par* 1; *SBOp* 6:261.

of the king becomes dissatisfied with good and leaves paradise for an evil world. Again, the saint stresses the importance of not taking for granted the grace of free choice. The freedom of choice is for humans to make, but the act is not purely natural, for the *imago Dei* in our being serves as a grace to guide individuals to make good choices. Bernard understands that effective soul direction comes only through the mutual submission of both parties involved. An individual's development into Christlikeness can be directed but not forced.

Letter 91 to the Abbots Assembled at Soissons (1132)

Following the example of the Cistercians' General Chapter each year, the Benedictine abbots in the province of Rheims decided to meet annually at Soissons. They invited Bernard to attend their initial meeting; a request he was unable to fulfill. In his stead, he sent a letter to the abbots, praising their reforming spirit, and encouraging them to have strength to carry on the reform, despite the difficulties. Bernard urges these reforming abbots not to meet simply for the sake of meeting, but to strive to make good and righteous not only what they do, but in their lives, as well. In other words, who they are is as important as any reforms they enact. This will disarm those who would want to mock them in the future for meeting for nothing.

In what seems to be reminiscent of his steps of humility and pride, Bernard likens their reforming process to climbing a ladder. One can move up or down the ladder, but staying still only brings instability, leading to a fall. These abbots must continue their reforming zeal or else abandon it. They cannot attempt to maintain the *status quo*. These abbots, whose assembly will undoubtedly will draw criticism, must remember the salvation of their spiritually young, and not focus on the murmurs of the spiteful. By focusing on what is good for them, and not just what they want, these abbots will fulfill their duty of being the *abbates* of their spiritual *fili*. Their faithfulness could have a purifying effect on the entire church.

Rather than suggesting that these abbots temper their reform, Bernard encourages them to forge ahead with their reforms, knowing that it is their obligation to bring others along with them. It is duty that summons Bernard to encourage these abbots to seek reform. For Bernard, reform begins with each individual who fulfills his or her assigned obligation to God through the church. Merely meeting in Chapter once a year will not suffice to enact Benedictine reform. Each of these abbots must live reformed lives.

This takes sacrifice, and dealing with those who are hesitant can lead to discouragement, but these abbots know what the spiritually immature need, and they must follow-through and "faithfully drag the reluctant to God."[15]

LETTERS TO WILLIAM OF ST. THIERRY

William of St. Thierry was perhaps Bernard's closest friend, and Bernard openly acknowledged their affection for one another. This close relationship gave Bernard the freedom to release his inner feelings in his correspondence with William. These letters are enlightening to read, and demonstrate, among other things, his ability to become easily frustrated with someone he dearly loves.

In *Letter 85* (1125), Bernard takes offense from William's assertion in a previous letter that Bernard's love for William is less than William's love for Bernard. Showing his playfulness with language, Bernard confesses that William might think that Bernard's love for him is less than his love for Bernard, but he playfully asserts, "I am certainly certain that you aren't certain." The reason for this, Bernard argues, is that love requires self-knowledge. However teasing William's letter may have been, his humor has uncovered a more serious issue at hand. Since William's humorous complaint was based on an assumption that William knows Bernard's heart, it demonstrates that William does not really know himself.[16] Bernard becomes quite agitated with William as the letter continues, and suggests that William feels this way because Bernard has not answered his many letters. He regains his composure, however, and admits that William is perhaps correct, for Bernard is only able to love with the limited capacity that God has given him. Bernard does not promise an eternal love to William, for as a human he does not possess that capability. The language expressed in this letter is ripe with irony. These two men have a deep affection for each other, so they feel free to write whatever comes to their minds. The close relationship between the two abbots was one of mutual spiritual direction. They could share freely with one another without concern for rhetorical precision or political maneuvering; rather the joy of rhetorical play. Their mutual love for Christ and commitment to monastic reform was the formation of their bond. Their similar personalities sealed it.

15. *Ep* 305; *SBOp* 8:241.
16. See McGuire, *Friendship & Community*, 252–53.

In *Letter 86* (1125), Bernard addresses William's desire to leave the Benedictines for the Cistercians and become a monk under Bernard at Clairvaux. In other letters to abbots who desired a different assignment, Bernard scolds them for desiring to leave their monks fatherless. What makes this letter interesting is its contradicting nature from other letters Bernard wrote to individuals who sought the 'higher way.' Instead of commending William for seeking a Cistercian profession, he encourages his friend to remain at St. Thierry.

He writes that he has known of William's desire to become a Cistercian for a long time, but he cannot recommend that William follow-through on this desire, for he does not have the physical ability to live a Cistercian lifestyle. Bernard acknowledges that they both wish that William could move to Clairvaux, but he has to advise William in the way that he thinks God desires. This letter is spiritual direction at its elemental state. Bernard's intention is to counsel William in the way that God would counsel William. William should seek the God-intended ideal for his life, and not what he perceives to be his own desires.

In his heart, Bernard understands that a Clairvaux with William would not be advantageous for either of them.[17] Both the distance between them and their distinct Orders offer a way for them to share each other's lives objectively. Furthermore, the personalities of these two men were too similar, creating a potentially disastrous situation if they both resided in Clairvaux. For example, they both had impulsive tendencies and wrote in a similar style and with similar subject matter.[18] Because Bernard had the discernment and wisdom to understand himself, their relationship, and the hazards of this potential situation, he disapproved of William's desire to enter Clairvaux. In what appears to be a compromise in Williams's mind (although it still met with the disapproval of Bernard) William became a Cistercian monk at the Abbey of Signy, where he spent the rest of his life.

LETTER 523 TO ÆLRED OF RIEVAULX (1142)

Ælred, known as the "Bernard of the North" for his similar approach to the spiritual life, was another of Bernard's dearest friends. He was the third abbot of the Rievaulx monastery, and completely English. Ælred was a remarkable figure. At the age of twenty, he became a clerk and later a

17. Leclercq, "Lettres de S. Bernard Introduction," 53.

18. Stiegman, "Bernard of Clairvaux, William of St. Thierry, The Victorines," 140–42.

high steward in the court of King David of Scotland. Four years later, he entered the new Cistercian abbey of Rievaulx. He became the abbot of the monastery in Revesby, Lincolnshire before returning to Rievaulx as its abbot. Under his benevolent nature and genuine holiness, the Rievaulx abbey grew to more than 600 monks. His influence in monastic England rivaled Bernard's influence on the European mainland, but Ælred had much more experience and ease in the courts than did his friend to the south. Bernard and Ælred were close because not only did they share the same monastic goals, but since they since they shared comparable monasteries and influence, they could empathize with one another. One wonders why Bernard could have this level of collegial comfort with the Cistercian Ælred, but not with William of St. Thierry, whom Bernard discouraged from becoming a Cistercian. Perhaps the English Channel provided a necessary comfort zone for the abbot of Clairvaux.

Bernard's only surviving letter to his dear friend appears as anything but friendly, not providing any evidence (other than irony) that these two abbots had a close relationship at all. Bernard had asked Ælred to compose a treatise on love. After a period of time, no such treatise appeared. In this letter, Bernard scolds his friend for not obeying him. In escalating language, Bernard says, "I have asked you—no, I have instructed you. Rather, I have charged you by oath in the name of God to write a little something for me . . ." In a self-effacing manner, Ælred believed he was too intimidated to write such a treatise, for he felt that he did not possess the spiritual depth necessary to complete the task. Bernard confronts his older friend for not exhibiting humility by consenting to his request, and in a backhanded way calls Ælred's stubbornness a form of idolatry with the words of 1 Samuel 15:23: "It is like the sin of divination, and like the crime of idolatry, to refuse to obey."

As the letter progresses, Bernard becomes so frustrated with Ælred that he commands him in the name of Jesus Christ and the Spirit of God to write a treatise on charity. Bernard offers to help him get started by even giving it a name: *The Mirror of Charity*. He orders Ælred to place this letter as its preface, so that if readers do not like it, they can blame Bernard, and not Ælred, for its composition.

Without a prior knowledge of the close relationship between these two abbots, one might discern that Bernard cared very little for Ælred. However, when understood as a letter written with wry wit and sarcasm, the close relationship between these two men becomes more apparent. The importance of this letter lies (in addition to its recipient) in the confidence Bernard had in God's ability to work through others. Bernard saw in Ælred an elder friend who had spent many years working skillfully in the in the courts of England, but he also saw in his friend the capacity for much more. This treatise would be a spiritual exercise for Ælred, who would come to understand himself in a clearer way through the composition of this work. The hyperbole inherent in this letter is Bernard's attempt at getting his friend's attention. Bernard knew how Ælred would receive the letter, and he was correct; *The Mirror of Charity* was published by Ælred with Bernard's letter as the preface.

CONCLUSIONS

The letters of Bernard to abbots are difficult to discern. Bernard was an abbot as they were, but he was much more than an abbot. For the Cistercians he served as an *abbas principis*: the heart and soul of the Order, and (rightly or wrongly) the example for others to follow. For those outside the Cistercian Order, Bernard must have been seen as a paradox: an abbot who had a literal understanding of St. Benedict's *Rule*, yet due to his many worldly involvements, made convenient exceptions regarding the *Rule* in his own abbacy.

Despite any inconsistencies in his own role at Clairvaux, Bernard's letters to his fellow abbots are written with spiritual authority. As an abbot himself, his standards for them were high. Through them, Bernard demonstrates his values for all abbots, regardless of their Order. First, abbots are fathers to their monks, and their first concern must be their spiritual welfare. God has given abbots the spiritual custody of their sons. Abbots who do not recognize this responsibility are placing the souls of their monks in jeopardy. The primary means to accomplish this is for abbots to have a healthy self-understanding and awareness of God in their own lives. They must guard their own souls before they can take responsibility for the souls of others. Second, abbots must be content with their present situation until God calls them elsewhere. Self-serving abbots who are constantly seeking either greater or lesser appointments are disappointing Almighty God, for they do not represent a serving Christ, but a selfish sinner. Abbots must not forget although they are spiritual fathers, they are still obedient sons of God. Self-ambition is a foreign ideal for professed monks, for they have given their vocational rights to Christ through obedience to their monastic

Order. Finally, realizing that their monasteries represent God to the temporal society, abbots must maintain the highest of standards regarding relationships with the outside world. How they deal with outsiders will affect their spiritual lives, regardless if they are either peasants or kings. The faithfulness of the abbots will promote the faithfulness of the monastery, which will promote the faithfulness of the Order, monasticism, the church, and finally the world.

These three duties of an abbot reflect the very life of Christ himself. Laying down their desires, aspirations, and lives by choosing a cross is the essence of faithfulness to God for any Christian. Abbots were elected and given both temporal and spiritual authority by their monks through the direction of the Holy Spirit. Monastic reform was in their control. Understanding the letters of Bernard of Clairvaux to abbots are essential for understanding his monastic desires for the church in his age and his understanding of the process of directing souls.

CHAPTER 6

The Letters of Bernard to Bishops

FOR BERNARD, THE BISHOPS of the church were vital to its spiritual health, but they were not above reproach. Although medieval bishops spent a great deal of energy engaged in the politics of their diocese, Bernard consistently judged them on their moral and spiritual character. In the many episcopal elections in which Bernard intervened, his support was always for the candidate he believed had the highest moral character. When possible, in situations such as the Archbishop of York affair in 1140, Bernard always supported a Cistercian candidate, whom he believed would always be the more spiritual of the episcopal candidates. Interestingly, of the Cistercian bishops elected in the first half of the twelfth-century, three-fourths had at one time been monks of Clairvaux.[1]

In his more than eighty letters to bishops and archbishops, Bernard demonstrates respect for his ecclesiastical authorities, yet he never avoids offering counsel or correction when he deems it necessary. Although bishops held places of authority over abbots, Bernard often took the role of a spiritual father in his written communication with them. Medieval bishops had considerable power over monasteries, so like other abbots, Bernard had to take care when writing them. Bishops had the power to excommunicate monks, confirm or remove an abbot, and render discipline when necessary. Most of his letters to members of the episcopacy are formal in nature, with obligatory introductions and courtesies common to forms found in many versions of the medieval epistolary protocol known as the *ars dictaminis*.

Regarding the election of bishops, Bernard did not hesitate becoming involved, particularly during a dispute between two or more candidates.

---

1. Lipkin, "The Entrance of the Cistercians into the Church Hierarchy," 65–6.

Bernard believed a bishop's moral character, even his motivations, were more important than any administrative prowess he may possess. Bernard had a desire to ensure that those who shared his reformation goals and who had a moral character (according to Bernard's standards) were elected bishops.

Although Bernard wrote many letters to bishops, his involvement in their affairs was minimal. His letters dealt primarily with their moral and spiritual obligations, intervention on behalf of others, or responding to their request for his counsel on a given matter. Only rarely and under extreme circumstances (albeit extreme as determined by Bernard himself) did he urge them to act in a particular manner. According to Bernard, bishops had their own trials to endure, including evils that lurked within their own household.[2] The best Bernard could do was offer spiritual counsel to help them discern and judge situations before them. Despite the fact that Bernard himself refused the episcopacy when it was offered to him, he does not hesitate to offer counsel to bishops on how they should govern their dioceses. While this chapter can in no way analyze every epistle Bernard wrote to bishops, several of them in this collection represent the character and nature of his communication with those in the episcopacy.

LETTER 42, "BERNARD'S EPISCOPAL THEOLOGY" (1127–1128)

Bernard had definite understandings regarding the role and character of bishops. While he respected their authority, he did not hesitate to challenge them from time to time. Bernard believed a bishop's moral character was much more important than his administrative prowess, and he held them to this standard. In Sermon 76 of the *Song of Songs*, he writes, "Good and faithful shepherds never cease to fatten their flocks with good and excellent examples; from their own lives and not from the lives of others."[3] Rather than referring public morals and virtues to archdeacons and other attendants, bishops should set the moral example themselves. Bernard truly believed he possessed impartational wisdom from God that these bishops needed, and it was his divine responsibility to offer it to them.

Bernard's episcopal theology is developed most extensively in his letter to Henry, Archbishop of Sens, written around 1127. Sometimes

2. *SC* 77.3; *SBOp* 1:263.
3. *SC* 76.9; *SBOp* 1:259.

counted among his treatises rather than in the epistolary corpus, Bernard is responding to Henry, who had asked Bernard to write something for him. The work is an example of Bernard offering spiritual counsel to a bishop who has asked for guidance. In a statement of rhetorical humility, Bernard begins by discussing why a simple monk can address a bishop. Bernard contrasts the unassuming lives of monks with that of the opulence of those in the episcopacy but reminds Henry of their similarity in that both monks like himself and bishops like Henry are priests. Because of this vocational similarity, Bernard feels comfortable to address Henry in this letter.

He praises Henry for reforms he has enacted and for having the wisdom to surround himself with honorable counselors. Throughout the first section of this letter, Bernard refers to Henry not as a bishop but as a priest. By reminding Henry of his first calling, Bernard attempts to get to the very core of Henry's desire to be a bishop. Although the grandeur of his surroundings has changed, Henry has not. Despite the many pressures facing him, he should always desire to please God rather than others. In a play on words, he writes, "If you desire to please people, you don't please God. If you don't please him, you don't appease him."

In the second part of this letter/treatise, Bernard discusses the importance of chastity, charity, and humility in the life of a priest. Chastity keeps the body and mind of the priest restrained, as his focus is on Christ within him rather than on the temptations around him. Charity toward others flows from a pure heart, a clear conscience, and an undying faith in Christ. Through charity, a priest represents Christ's ideals in the world. The spiritual lesson here is that internal formation in Christ results in an outer representation of Christ. Humility is the virtue providing fortification for chastity and charity against the temptations of the world. Bernard admits that he knows not why the Trinitarian Godhead associates most intimately with the virtue of humility, but God chose Christ to appear to humanity in the lowly form of Jesus.[4] He writes that for bishops, humility is most important, for what looks like honors to those who aspire to the bishopric are actually burdens. Bishops who have a healthy understanding of themselves will be able to endure the opulent temptations around them.

Finally, Bernard compares the issue of monastic exemptions from episcopal authority with individual spiritual accountability. Bernard was highly critical of monasteries that desired freedom from local bishopric

---

4. In *The Steps of Humility and Pride*, Bernard writes that Christ possessed all of the virtues, but he commends humility most of all. *Hum* 9.25; *SBOp* 3:36.

control and have accountability only to the pope. He writes of himself that if he ever desired to shake the yoke of his own bishop from around his neck, "it would not be long before I subjected myself to the tyranny of Satan." Growth in Christ does not come in isolation, but within the fellowship and communion of those in the church. Separation from others, and the accountability that results from mutual lives in Christ, does not foster self-understanding, but self-deception. In this lengthy letter, Bernard impresses upon this important archbishop not to forget himself in the midst of the many trials around him. Without his silken garments, Henry was a simple priest of Christ. Beneficial to him would be the presence of others who could be honest in assisting Henry to have a healthy understanding of himself.

Bernard's episcopal theology is grounded in the idea that the church is only as faithful as those appointed by Christ to lead the church. Bishops should seek not power but humility. They should concern themselves with the pastoral care of those in their diocese. They should exhibit modesty in lifestyle as a demonstration of their commitment to Christ and not to the cares of the world. Bernard understood that bishops faced innumerable temptations for wealth, power, and prestige. He also believed that bishops had a spiritual responsibility to those in their diocese to seek Christ and not selfish ambition. As an abbot serves as a spiritual father to his monks, bishops serve as a secular abbot to the Christians in his diocese. The spiritual well-being of the laity, priests, and monks was the responsibility of those in episcopal leadership.

EARLY EPISCOPAL COUNSEL: LETTERS TO NEW BISHOPS

Bernard's desire in writing letters to new bishops in the early 1130s was to offer spiritual counsel to them before found themselves in need of correction. *Letters 25–28* are brief letters, written to offer counsel to those who were entering a phase in life different from anything else they had ever experienced. In these letters, the abbot offers counsel and admonitions regarding their spiritual lives, the manner of their rule, and the people under their rule. Following the example of Gregory the Great, Bernard exhorts these bishops that before they can rule others, they must first be ruled by Christ themselves.

Letter 26 to Guy, Bishop of Lausanne (1130)

In this very brief and seemingly unimportant letter, written in the form of a quick memo, Bernard offers counsel to a distant cousin named Guy, the newly elected bishop in Lausanne. Lacking much of his usual epistolary style, this letter demonstrates Bernard's ability to summarize his position on an issue quickly, not wasting a single word in the text. Each of the four sentences corresponds with one of the four cardinal virtues: fortitude, prudence, justice, and temperance, and three of the four sentences are paraphrases of distinct passages of Scripture. Through a series of responsibilities and personal virtues to achieve these tasks, Bernard offers a twofold exhortation to Guy: to respect his ecclesiastical duty and to rule himself in addition to the people under him. This short note demonstrates a unique bond exists between ecclesiastical and personal discipline for Bernard. The potential of this holy union is the faithfulness and reform of the church.

In the first sentence, representing fortitude, Bernard acknowledges Guy has sought this appointment: "You have put your hand to great things, so you need strength." This appointment was not a surprise to Guy, but a position he aspired to hold. Guy is going to need great strength to be a good bishop, but it may not be the strength Guy expects. As the only sentence in this letter not explicitly connected to a passage of Scripture, this statement bears distinction.

The second line of this short letter is reminiscent of Ezekiel 3:17. Bernard writes, "You have become a watchman on the houses of Israel, so you need prudence." While the Ezekiel passage makes no mention of the cardinal virtue of Prudence, it does include a caveat: "Son of man, I have made you a watchman for the house of Israel; so hear the word I speak and give them a warning from me." As a watchman over the Lausanne diocese, Guy is called both to hear the word of God and then to speak on God's behalf. He is to demonstrate prudence in his life by knowing what to do and how to do it. In a way, the demonstration of prudence is exactly what Bernard is doing through this letter. He feels compelled to write Guy with a warning from God. Rather then sending Guy a note typical of the many congratulatory letters he must have surely received from all over the church, Bernard is demonstrating prudence through a carefully written exhortational summons. Guy must now demonstrate the virtue in his own life by the courses of action he will take as a bishop.

The third sentence of the letter is from Romans 1:14, which states, "I am obligated both to Greeks and non-Greeks, both to the wise and the foolish." This statement may represent the universal aspect of Guy's calling. Bernard writes, "You are indebted to both the wise and the foolish, so you need justice." Guy does not preside over either the wise or the foolish; he is one indebted to them.[5] While the virtue of justice is a primary focus of this sentence, it also serves to remind Guy of the servanthood of his position. He is God's representative to the people of Lausanne, called to serve each one of them.

In the final sentence, Bernard summarizes the letter with a warning, reminiscent of 1 Corinthians 9:27: "But I discipline my body and bring it into subjection, lest, when I have preached to others, I myself should become disqualified." He writes, "Finally, you must have self control most of all, let having preached to others, God forbid, you yourself become a reprobate." Temperance is a common theme in Bernard. From his earliest writings to his *Sermons on the Song of Songs*, Bernard maintains having control of oneself by understanding one's motivations and desires is the surest way to perfect love for God. In this letter, Bernard is advocating a practical mysticism, in which Guy lives in obedience to God by his divine calling, lived out as prudence, justice, and self-discipline.[6] If Guy aspires to be a bishop, he must realize that if he is not careful, he may lose himself and the spiritual progress he has made to this point in his life.

In addition to advocating the inward dwelling of the cardinal virtues in Guy's life, these four straightforward sentences can be summarized in two basic exhortations. The first regards vocation: Guy must respect his position as a bishop. The second regards the personal: Guy must respect his own salvation. As the structure of Bernard's sentences suggests, these two realities are intimately intertwined. A bond exists between ecclesiastical and personal discipline. He has put his hand to great things, so he needs great strength. He is a watcher over the houses of Israel, so he needs prudence. He has a duty to all, so he needs justice. Failure to accomplish each of these divine mandates may result in his downfall.

Whether or not Guy accepted Bernard's counsel is debatable. He was a supporter of Cistercian causes in the diocese, but this benefice seems to be the extent of his financial charity. However, from the deplorable state of the

5. Bernard uses this same language in *Ep* 55 to Geoffrey, Bishop of Chartres.

6. I distinguish Bernard's "practical mysticism" from the mysticism of the Carthusians or Premonstratensians, which stressed contemplative mystical experience. For Bernard, the goal of mystical union with God is love for others, not simply a mystical union with God for the sake of oneself. However, the differentiation between these two ideals is subtle.

diocese upon the ascension of Amadeus of Lausanne, Guy apparently left an administration ripe with scandals.

Letters 27 and 28 to Ardutio, Bishop-Elect of Geneva (1135–1136)

In his letters to Ardutio, Bernard shares the same counsel he did with Guy, but with an addendum: To save both his integrity and his soul, he should surround himself with men of good counsel. From the tone of these letters, Bernard seems to have known Ardutio well, or at least his reputation. Why Bernard wrote these letters, and their significance, lie not only in his desire to offer spiritual guidance to Ardutio, but also in Bernard's anthropological assumptions and their implications for the church.

Letter 27 is very carefully written. The Latin is complex and the subject matter not explicitly succinct. Bernard warns the bishop-elect not to think too highly of himself or his abilities, or his exaltation will end up collapsing on him. He must remember it was the grace of God, and not Ardutio's abilities, that allowed him to be elected. In this letter, Bernard describes an inner qualification for someone who is assuming the bishopric. He tells Ardutio, "Make sure your heart and devotion are right and your ministry holy. If you weren't holy before, make sure you are now!" This concept of holiness in the life of a bishop is essential to Bernard's understanding of who an episcopal leader should be. A bishop who exemplifies holiness is a bishop who embodies the very essence of Christ. Bernard prays Ardutio will not rely on his own strength or the prestige of his office, but as Christ did on earth, display humility in spite of his great power. This begins with inner confession, which was seen by many in Bernard's lifetime as a healthy way to look at oneself in preparation for redemptive grace. An acknowledgement of sin and a movement towards repentance brings joy from God, not false joy offered by the world. Thus, for Bernard, in addition to a preparation for redemption, confession also serves as a means of experiencing God's grace as it draws one closer to God. To ensure faithfulness, Ardutio must inaugurate his episcopal service with honest confession to God of his sins and motivations.

In Letter 28, written to Ardutio just after the new bishop had assumed the office, Bernard's language (if not his sentence structure) is clearer and more straightforward than in Letter 27. He begins the letter stating that his love for Ardutio gives him the confidence to speak to him with boldness. Bernard confesses that before his election, he could not discern in Ardutio's life many of the virtues required for a bishop. He writes, "Your past spirit did not at all seem to go with the duties of a bishop. But what of this? Can't God raise up a child of Abraham from this stone?" This reference to John the Baptist's proclamation in Matthew 3:9 is meant to encourage Ardutio in that despite his limited espiscopal qualification, even God can perform a miracle in his life.

Bernard tries to encourage Ardutio to look at the examples of Paul, Matthew, Ambrose, and others who came from a worldly life to a prominent place of leadership in the church. The abbot encourages the bishop to put behind him the offenses of his youth (*delicta iuventutis*) and to become the godly man God wants him to be by honoring the ministry God has called him to assume. This honest confession of Bernard's initial impression of Ardutio must have been difficult for the bishop to read, but Bernard felt it was necessary to write more succinctly in this letter than in the first. He exhorts Ardutio that because he has limited gifts for the bishopric, he should surround himself with others who might assist him. "Have honorable men in council, honorable men in your service, and have honorable men in your house. They will guard your life and integrity, and be witnesses of it." Isolation from virtuous people is a sure means to temptation and pride.

This counsel reflects Bernard's anthropological understanding of self-knowledge. If Ardutio has an honest comprehension of himself, he will realize he needs people around him to offer him support and counsel. Relying on the fact he is in a position of power will not in itself enable him to be a good bishop. He must first see himself as God sees him, and only then will he know how to preside over the people of Geneva. Through these two letters to Ardutio, Bernard emphasizes to the new bishop that the most important aspect of his bishopric is his understanding of himself, his role as a bishop, and the responsibility of the diocese in the work of the church on earth. These sequential priorities would foster a healthy diocese, leading to the spiritual health of the entire church.

LETTERS OF VOCATIONAL COUNSEL

LETTERS TO MALACHY

One of Bernard's dearest friends (if only in reformation zeal) was Archbishop Malachy O'Morgair of Ireland. While ecclesiastical leaders in Ireland did not always welcome Malachy's monastic and ecclesiastic reforms, he was tireless in his attempts to extirpate barbarism and restore Christian morals and obedience to Rome. Malachy had deep respect for Bernard and was instrumental in the foundation of a Cistercian abbey in Ireland. Upon return from a trip to Rome in 1148, Malachy visited Clairvaux but succumbed to an illness and died there.

In *Letter 341* (1140) Bernard is responding to a letter he received from Malachy in which the archbishop requested two Irish monks from Clairvaux to make a foundation in Ireland. While Bernard agrees these specific monks would be ideal candidates for the task, he tells Malachy that both he and his brethren in Clairvaux agree the two are not spiritually ready for such an endeavor. The abbot encourages Malachy in the interim to search for a suitable site for a foundation, so when the monks are ready, they will have a place to go.

What makes this letter significant is the instruction Bernard gives to Malachy, who served both as the Archbishop of Ireland and as a Legate of Rome. He writes, "I beg you to preach the holy word of the Lord, to give people the knowledge of their salvation." Bernard is arguing that since Malachy serves as both an archbishop and a papal legate, his commitments should be twofold. Although the task of an archbishop and a legate require many administrative and political duties, Bernard focuses on Malachy's call to preach not to the dignified in society but to the *plebi*, or common people. Bernard exhorting Malachy to remember the spiritual needs of all people when preaching is reminiscent of the instruction of Gregory the Great, who emphasizes the importance of diversity in preaching in order to speak to the needs of all people under a pastor's care.[7] An individual with Malachy's authority should not forget these forgotten ones. Including himself with this group of people, Bernard closes the letter by asking for Malachy's prayers.

Several months later, Bernard finally allowed the Irish monks of Clairvaux to establish a foundation in their homeland. *Letter 356* (1141) seems to have been carried by these monks to Malachy. In the letter, Bernard refers to the monks as "*seminis*," or seeds. He writes regarding these men, "I have sown, you increase, and God gives the harvest." Both he and Malachy have a place in directing the souls of these monks. Malachy's ecclesiastical position does not release him from this spiritual responsibility. Bernard creates a communion of spiritual enrichment for these monks. Their spiritual

7. *Pastoral Rule* 3.36.

development requires more than just one influencing person in their lives. Bernard, Malachy, and God all have a part in their growth in Christ. Had not Bernard and Malachy done their part, then God would not have the opportunity to grow them in the faith. Rather than understanding the role of humanity as being weak and helpless before God, and although he clearly acknowledges the reality of original sin and the frailty of humankind, Bernard places importance on the role of the individual as partners with God's activities on earth. The process of directing souls transpires through the efforts of humanity, as well as the action of the Holy Spirit. God blesses the efforts of individuals, however slight, as they strive toward spiritual maturity, either in their own lives or in the lives of others.

LETTER 319 TO THURSTAN, ARCHBISHOP OF YORK (1139)

This letter represents those written by Bernard in which he insists that a person appointed to a particular place of service in the church should demonstrate obedience through stability. Bernard had high regard for Thurstan, for in *Letter 95*, he praises Thurstan for his reforming zeal and holy life. In *Letter 319*, Bernard is responding to a request for counsel from an aging Thurston, who was pondering a decision to resign his archbishopric in order to die in a monastery.

Although Bernard praises Thurston's desire for quiet and to rest in the Lord, he cannot see a sufficient excuse for Thurstan to abnegate his office. According to Bernard, two reasons exist for a bishop to abandon his office: the commission of a grave sin or crime or license from the pope. Since Thurston has not named either of these, Bernard cannot suggest that he resign. Nevertheless, Bernard does have a compromise for him. Thurstan should stay where he his but "exhibit in a bishop the garment and humble life of a monk." If Thurstan is really seeking a monastic life, he does not need to enter a monastery at this time to follow the monastic ideal. If Thurstan wanted to spend his final days in a monastery due to his own spiritual doubts and eternal insecurities, Bernard is releasing him from these fears.

This letter bestows two significant insights into Bernard's vocational theology. In his citation of two acceptable reasons for resigning the episcopacy, he offers one reason dealing with internal virtues and a second relating to external obedience. These two ideals form a faithful servant of Christ in the church. Both are necessary for Thurstan to fulfill his vocational calling.

The archbishop could remain in York out of simple obedience to the Pope, but without a pure heart, he will not be fulfilling his call to *curae pastorali*.

The second vocational insight this letter offers is the monastic charism need not transpire within the confines of a monastery. Although Bernard writes the monastery is the surest means to heaven, humble servants of Christ can live the monastic paradigm wherever they reside. An individual follows the monastic ideal by focusing more on his or her life and character than on a habit or tonsure. For example, in the *Apologia*, Bernard refers to a double unhappiness for those who carry Christ's cross without following after him, for they are sharing in Christ's sufferings without regard for imitating Christ's humility.[8] Monastic faithfulness involves far more than affiliation. It requires an inner conformity to the ideals of Christ. Although Bernard believed that the entire church would benefit from monastic reformation, the reformation in Bernard's mind was far deeper than merely constructing monastic cloisters.

Letter 372 to Peter, Bishop of Palencia in Spain (1146–1147)

In response to a letter from Bishop Peter extolling the praises of the abbot of Clairvaux, Bernard responds with an insightful and important letter regarding self-awareness and the nature and function of praise and humility. Bernard begins the letter with pompous flattery of Peter and compares him to the virtues contained in no less than twelve passages of Scripture in the first six sentences. He relates how he has received word of "your lofty spirit, of your love for reading, of your gentle manner, and of the good you do to all, but especially to the household of the faithful."

Despite this adulation, Bernard writes that he in no way desires to praise Peter, but to spare him from praise. Since he is a sinner, praise would only anoint him with an oil of a sinner. Instead, Peter needs an oil of joy, which comes from a pure heart, a good conscience, and a true faith. Praise, Bernard argues, is not due to the created but to the Creator.

In this section of the letter, Bernard offers an unambiguous description of the importance of understanding the self. "Man is both a rational and mortal creature," Bernard wrote to a young man who had promised himself to the monastic life, "One we are by the grace of our Creator, the other by the consequence of our sin."[9] This dual placement in God's created

8. *Apo* 2; *SBOp* 3:82.
9. *Ep* 412; *SBOp* 8:394.

order places humanity in a unique position. Humanity has the capacity for godliness, but humanity lost it due to a misuse of the gift of reason. The human journey from created, to fallen, to redeemed underscores Bernard's understanding of what it means to be human. Because God created humanity in God's image and likeness, each person has worth and value to God. Because each person has value and worth, an examination of the self is a worthwhile exercise. Self-knowledge, according to Bernard, consists in three things: knowing what we have done in the past, knowing what we deserve from God, and knowing what we have lost through our sin.[10] Self-knowledge is an awareness of our sinful nature, which leads to hope for a change in our condition.[11] In order to understand ourselves correctly, and humbly, we must accept our current state that resulted from the Fall. In *The Steps of Humility and Pride*, Bernard writes that in order to understand oneself, one must first set up a ladder of humility in the heart in order to obtain a healthy view.[12] Pride is clear evidence that someone has not fully arrived at self-understanding, for true self-understanding results in humility of heart and life, for when a person sees the sinful reality of one's state, humility is the result.

Bernard writes to Bishop Peter that some people are knowingly ignorant of the gifts God has given them for fear of becoming full of pride and then falling into the devil's trap if they pay attention to these gifts. Bernard explains it is a good thing to know what the Lord has given him so he also knows what he lacks. "Anyone who has received a gift and doesn't know what they have received stands in twofold danger of being ungrateful for what he has received and careless in not guarding it." When one obtains knowledge regarding how God has gifted that person, he or she is charged with guarding that gift. By offering this counsel to Bishop Peter, Bernard is assisting the bishop in the process of self-discovery and the stewardship of his God-bestowed gifts.

Following Bernard's reasoning, for a Christian to ignore the gifts God has given him or her is irresponsible. Appreciating these gifts is not pride, but a realization of how one is formed in the image of God. This understanding leads to a healthy anthropological perspective. Pride is the result of not fully comprehending one's giftedness, one's motives, or one's place on earth. It stems from a false understanding of oneself, in which he or she wrongly

---

10. *Div* 40.3; *SBOp* 6/1:236.

11. McGinn, "Freedom, Formation and Reformation," 91–114.

12. *Hum* 15; *SBOp* 3:27–8.

believes that gifts are the creation of humanity. In Bernard's own words, "Humility is a virtue whereby a man has a bad opinion of himself because he understands himself well."[13] In modern terminology, self-awareness is not an end in itself, but a means to an end, which is faithfulness to Christ. Knowing one's limitations allows the individual to appreciate with all humility that he or she is fully reliant on Christ.

Bernard summarizes his understanding of receiving praise through self-understanding with an analogy. He writes to Peter, "Faith is a pot, and a big one, so it can collect much grace. Its cover is fear, so the water of wisdom will not be stained with the filth of vainglory." A fear of God from understanding one's weaknesses and helplessness before God is the surest way to accept praise when it is due, yet without becoming filled with the idolatry of pride. Bernard did not want to accept general praise from Bishop Peter. He would accept praise for specific instances when he used the gifts God had given him. Unlike other letter writers, who offered praise to Peter simply because he was a bishop, Bernard was not praising him, for in refraining from such general praise he was sparing the bishop from the temptation of sinful pride. Thus, the very nature of this letter was a means directing the soul of this bishop. For Bernard, this would undoubtedly have had an effect on the church, which could benefit from Peter's heightened awareness of God in his life.

LETTERS OF INTERVENTION

Bernard was not shy about making specific requests to bishops. Several of these petitions were made on behalf of someone else, usually the letter-bearer. Although he may not have personally met the bishop to whom he was writing, he confidently assumed that the bishop would know him and, based on his holy reputation, grant the request he was making in the letter.

Letter 62 to Henry, Bishop of Verdun (before 1129)

Bishop Henry had a turbulent bishopric, and because his acquaintance with Bernard was close, Bernard felt obliged to offer his assistance in Henry's affairs. Henry had been accused of corrupt financial transactions with the funds of the church. When he asked his close friend Bernard what he

13. *Hum* 1.2; *SBOp* 3:17.

should do, Bernard suggested that in order to avoid scandal, Henry should resign, which he did at a council at Châlons-sur-Marne in 1129. Because of Bernard's involvement in Henry's decision, unknown persons in the Roman Curia began to complain Bernard was interfering in the affairs of others. Bernard heard of this discontent in the Curia, and felt the necessity to defend himself. This self-defense resulted in *Letter 48* to Cardinal Haimeric, Chancellor of the Holy See, which is one the few letters Bernard wrote explicitly on his own behalf.

This brief letter to Henry, written sometime before 1129, demonstrates Bernard's spiritual interest in persons from all strata of society. Bernard is sending this letter with a woman who desperately needs Henry's help. She had been living in sin and was now estranged from her husband. Out of desperation she had sought Bernard's counsel and absolution. After advising and correcting her, he was now sending her back as a penitent to her bishop.

In the first line of this letter, Bernard refers to her as a *muliercula*. This term may reflect either derision or pity. As a medieval man, Bernard undoubtedly viewed women as the weaker gender, but not unequal in the eyes of Christ. Bernard saw this woman as a penitent sinner who desired to reconcile with God. The letter itself does not suggest that he reacted to her situation any differently than if she were a man. He was simply returning her to her spiritual shepherd.[14] Bernard clearly understood both his and her bishop's roles in her spiritual development.

The woman in question had taken the initiative in reconciling with God. Her motivations were honorable, even if her sins deplorable. Bernard seems pleased with how the woman has responded to his counsel, enabling her to return with confidence to the "bosom of her own shepherd." Because her motives are pure, Bernard counsels Henry not to reject her as a sinner but to accept her as a penitent. Bernard is able to offer this counsel due to his belief that the woman had taken appropriate steps to foster progression in her own spiritual growth.

Bernard believed the spiritual life of the individual contains three stages of growth: carnal, rational, and spiritual.[15] Each person enters these stages, but not all progress through them at the same rate, or even through

14. In a manner similar to the way he handled this situation with the penitent woman, several letters written to the abbots of runaway monks follow the same pattern. Bernard counseled them and then returned them to their abbots. E.g., *Epp* 399, 400, 406, and 413.

15. See *SC* 20; *SBOp* 1:114–21, and Pennington, "Three Stages of Spiritual Growth According to St. Bernard," 315–26.

them all. Human progression through these stages enhances and maintains one's faithfulness to and love for God. Bernard understood these stages in the practical life as relating to conversion, vocation, and contemplation. The movement through these life events can lead one to a life of holiness, although holiness is not a guarantee in this life, but freely chosen by the individual and divinely enabled by God. Faithfulness at any vocational level (pope, bishop, abbot, monk, or even *muliercula*), is accomplished when the individual is faithful to serve Christ at that capacity with a knowledge of self that leads to humility before Christ. Serving Christ without self-interest at any level leads to a life of holiness; however, because the three stages of spiritual growth are linked with one's vocation, the capacity for holiness is tempered.

In the last sentence of this letter, Bernard demonstrates his objectivity in dealing with this woman's situation by not naïvely believing the woman's story without substantiation. He writes to Henry that if this woman's sad story is true, either she must be reconciled to her former husband or they must both live single lives. While he has compassion and pity for her, he cannot assume everything she told him is truthful. He wants to believe her. He also has a deep understanding of human nature, and knows individuals will resort to unscrupulous practices in times of desperation. Regarding the human condition, Bernard was a pragmatist. Although he comes close to telling Henry how to respond, he leaves the situation to the bishop's judgment and discernment as to whether or not to believe her account.

Letter 64 to Alexander, Bishop of Lincoln (1129)

The First Crusade opened the way for members of the nobility to make pilgrimages to the Holy Land. The establishment of the Knights Templar in the early twelfth-century made the long journey more secure, particularly within the new kingdom of Jerusalem, as the early Templars served as guardians of those making the passage from the Middle East seaports to the city of Jerusalem. Members of the nobility and others made these pilgrimages for penance, for profit, out of curiosity, and to alleviate the guilt of sin.

In *Letter 64*, Bernard writes to Alexander, the Bishop of Lincoln, who had given his blessing to a young man named Philip to make a pilgrimage to Jerusalem. On the way, Philip stopped at Clairvaux, and while there felt called to become a monk.[16] Because his bishop had given him a blessing

16. Bernard had a reputation for his tremendous skill in recruiting new monks.

for his voyage to the Holy Land, Bernard writes Alexander to let him know what has transpired in this young man's life and to request that the bishop help the new monk settle his financial affairs back home. Of course, he cannot resist offering the bishop spiritual advice, as well, and warns him about keeping the glories of this life in perspective.

The significance of this letter is that it is one of the first instances when Bernard compares Clairvaux to Jerusalem. He begins the letter, "Your Philip who wanted to travel to Jerusalem has discovered a short cut and has arrived there very quickly . . . If you want to know, this is Clairvaux." Bernard then describes Clairvaux as Jerusalem due to the monks' "wholehearted devotion," "conformed life," and "spiritual family unity." The holiness of each monk has had a dramatically positive influence on the entire monastic community at Clairvaux. Bernard describes Clairvaux as the holy city, where Phillip is no longer an exile or alien in the world but an official citizen of Jerusalem. The ecclesiology inherent in this letter explicitly details Bernard's understanding of the Cistercian movement in the church and the exemplary witness of Clairvaux in this reformation. Clairvaux, the faithful Jerusalem, is representative of heaven itself, where the thoughts and efforts of everyone there are focused solely on glorifying God.

The grand imagery involved in this section of the letter serves to prepare the bishop for the real purpose of this epistle. Because Philip left the world unexpectedly, his financial affairs were not in order. He asks Bishop Alexander to secure his debts and to allow the house he had built for his mother on church lands to be hers until her death. After reading of Philip's glorious vocation, Bernard believed the bishop could not refuse these minor, worldly requests.

Bernard then turns to the bishop's own soul. The counsel he offers the bishop has nothing to do with his office or his tasks but instead, turns the bishop inward. He cautions Alexander not to love his possessions more than he loves himself, not to take flattery too seriously, and not to think death is far off in the future. The letter ends abruptly, with a sense of pending doom not unlike the final chapter of Isaiah, with description of death and agony.

While the structure and ending of this letter may appear to be unusual, in actuality Bernard is establishing a dual dichotomy between Clairvaux and the outside world, and between Philip's life in Jerusalem and the

---

When he traveled to Paris to preach at the university, several students followed him back to Clairvaux. See *Vita Prima*, 4.11.10.

bishop's life in Lincoln. Alexander's cathedral concerns the political affairs of society. Clairvaux exists for prayer and solitude before God. Philip is surrounded by holy people whose sole purpose is to glorify God. The people around Alexander are there to tempt him with selfish flattery and the reliance on possessions. Philip has chosen the better path. Alexander must warn against losing his soul in the midst of his own bishopric.

LETTERS OF AGENDA

As the abbot of a medieval monastery, Bernard should have had enough responsibilities to keep him busy. Moreover, as a Cistercian monk, fleeing the world for solitude, hard labor, and asceticism should have been enough to pacify his soul. For a man known for his legalistic, reformation monasticism, his understanding of what it meant to be a Cistercian monk was quite flexible, as his affairs into the issues of the day seemed to be in direct violation of his abbatial responsibilities. In *Letter 20* (1127–1128) to Haimeric, Cardinal Deacon, he provides justification for his many activities beyond Clairvaux, writing, "I consider nothing that concerns God as a matter of indifference to me." If an issue regarded God, Bernard took the issue upon himself. Engaging bishops into affairs Bernard deemed important was a delicate task. Bernard clearly had respect for the episcopal office, but in his role as the voice of God, Bernard also presumed they would act when he sounded an alarm.

LETTER 126 TO THE BISHOPS OF AQUITAINE (1131)

More than twenty letters exist in the letter corpus regarding the papal schism of the 1130s. Of these, only two were written to bishops. In his lengthy letter to the Aquitainian bishops of Limoges, Poitiers, Perigueux, and Saintes, Bernard expected them to heed his warning of the dangers of Gerard, Bishop of Angoulême. Gerard was known for his political acumen, and when Anti-Pope Anacletus promised Gerard legateship in return for his support, Gerard waited to see if Innocent would reciprocate the offer before officially supporting one or the other. Gerard's consideration of supporting Anacletus aggravated the abbot of Clairvaux, who sent the bishops an emotional harangue directed at Gerard.

The first sentence of the letter foreshadows what is to come: "Courage is gained in peace, proved in oppression, and confirmed in victory. Your time is now, and if you dare, do not lie hidden, do not be sluggish." He then criticizes Gerard's pride and position-seeking ambition. He confesses he is judging Gerard's heart based on suspicion rather than any specific data. Nevertheless, Bernard argues that Gerard's actions betray his inner motives, for as soon as Innocent was elected, Gerard applied for legateship. When he was refused, he sided with Anacletus.

In a long diatribe against Bishop Gerard, Bernard calls him (among other things) a man "without the fear of God or self respect," and a man who "is mocked and jeered by all those who are around him." Bernard has no respect whatsoever for Gerard, for in a time of tension and uncertainty in the church, Gerard's only concern is himself. This self-absorption and pride is what Bernard sees as wrong with the church. Just as an individual's growth in Christ affects the entire church, so does an individual's rejection of Christ. By painting Gerard as an *antichristum,* his attempt is to move the bishops of Aquitaine to action for the sake of the spiritual health of the church.

The letter then shifts from a diatribe against Gerard to the issue of the papal schism itself. The issue at hand is who should be the pope. The rightful pope should be the one with the good character, superior reputation, and the one with the more credible election.[17] According to Bernard, Innocent has all three. As shepherds of the church, the bishops have the responsibility to eradicate these evil men from power. Bernard chides bishops who seek the episcopal title but not the spiritual responsibility that accompanies it. In Bernard's view, bishops were an invaluable position in the church. Having served under the highly regarded William of Champeaux as a young monk and abbot no doubt influenced Bernard's high episcopal expectations. Bernard's interest in the matter is an attempt to shame the bishops into assuming the spiritual responsibility that is theirs by the very nature of their title.

Bernard closes the letter with statements of God's promises of comfort and strength in times of affliction. Their duty was to watch and take care of God's people so the people will not have stained hands. This understanding of episcopal responsibilities extends far beyond the political realm. The spiritual well being of the people in a bishop's diocese was linked directly to the bishop's faithfulness in office. He must remain strong in standing

---

17. The election was highly controversial, with many acknowledging that, although Innocent clearly had a better moral compass, Anacletus may have had the more legitimate election.

against those who sought to divert his attention from the spiritual to the political. Bernard's counsel serves as an example of the spiritual authority the bishops should themselves assume.

Letter 329 to the Bishop of Limoges (1146)

Because not all bishops had godly reputations, at times Bernard felt it necessary to interfere for the sake of the church. In this letter, he writes to one bishop to solicit help in deposing another, corrupt bishop. Bernard had already written the pope about the scandalous bishop of Rodez, calling him a *monstra* who has no regard for the blood shed by Christ.[18] Bernard's tactic in getting the attention of the Bishop of Limoges is by beginning the letter with a statement that he is not writing on behalf of his own interests or to seek anything for himself. Instead, he is writing to the bishop for his own sake. Should the bishop not respond to Bernard's request that something be done about the Bishop of Rodez, his own reputation is at stake.

Throughout his letters, Bernard employs the use of promoting a guilty conscience within the reader through warnings, challenges, and appeals. In this letter, Bernard's language is no less manipulative: "Therefore, do not be inconsistent with yourself, but let your words and your works be consistent." Bernard's intent is to incite this bishop to action by challenging him spiritually. In conclusion, Bernard reminds the bishop not to get too close to this immoral bishop. Citing 1 Timothy 5:22, he warns the bishop to "keep a watch on your own soul and not to share in the sins of others." Since each person has the capacity to make free choices, the maintenance of one's salvation begins with oneself and one's rejection of temptations.

When one fails in his or her faithfulness to Christ, Bernard is quite clear that confession of sin and restoration to Christ are imperative. For Bernard, confession becomes a cleansing event, just as all virtues are strengthened by obedience.[19] True confession is composed of both penitence and praise: the confession of one's own evil and the praise of God's benefits. The saint follows the example of those in Scripture, particularly King David in the Psalms, as acts of confession that all Christians should emulate. The abbot himself was aware of his own need for confession, as in the retraction of *The Steps of Humility and Pride*, in which he admits a theological error in misinterpreting a passage from the Gospel of Mark

18. *Ep* 328; *SBOp* 8:264–265.
19. *Div* 40.2; *SBOp* 6/1:235.

regarding Christ's knowledge of the Last Judgment. Bernard seems quite embarrassed about the situation, because he can find no way to recover the erroneous copies of his work. He concedes, "The only recourse to remedy the situation is to make my confession."[20] Throughout his letters, Bernard rarely admits an error, making this retraction unique in his works.

Missing in the life of the scandalous Bishop of Rodez is inner confession. Acknowledgment of one's sins and God's praises leads one to fulfill the object of human charity, which is the love of one's neighbor. If a selfless love of God is an emulation of God's love for humanity, then love towards others is a natural expression of one's love for God. Thus, for Bernard the only way to love one's neighbor purely is first to love God. As one loves his or her neighbor, a love for God is deepened and enriched. Bernard writes that because love for God "cannot be perfected unless it is nourished and increased by the love of one's neighbor, it is necessary to love one's neighbor."[21] Thus, for one to state a personal love for God but does not demonstrate love toward others, the individual proves by his or her very actions a lack of love for God.[22] Love for one's neighbor involves the issue of justice, for love leads one out of oneself and to the needs of others. As a Cistercian, Bernard did not live in isolation from others but in solidarity with his monastic brothers.[23]

The Bishop of Limoges must guard his own soul so as not to be unjustifiably influenced by the Bishop of Rodez or his supporters. Not even bishops are beyond the capacity to lose their own souls. The focus on oneself to facilitate spiritual progress is not a self-referenced self-love, but a means to loving God to one's full potential, resulting in a divine experience.[24] While the Bishop of Rodez has corrupted his soul with greed and other vices, the Bishop of Limoges must work to prevent them from occurring in his own life. The concept of community and accountability enables Bernard to share freely with the Limoges bishop, as he knows that they are part of the same church.

---

20. *Hum*; SBOp 3:15.

21. *Sent* 1.21; SBOp 6/2:14.

22. *Ep* 11.8; SBOp 7:58–9.

23. Olivera, "Aspects of the Love of Neighbor in the Spiritual Doctrine of Saint Bernard (II)," 226.

24. *Dil* 10.27; SBOp 3:142.

CONCLUSIONS

Bernard's letters to bishops demonstrates the importance he placed on their role in the Body of Christ. As shepherds, their duty was to care for and administrate the sheep in their flock and to keep that flock from imminent spiritual dangers. Rather than viewing their position as a lofty blessing, bishops should instead feel the weight of their responsibilities, both temporal and spiritual.

Bernard clearly had respect for episcopal authority, particularly when bishops were faithful to their tasks. Even regarding malignant bishops, the abbot still addressed them as his superiors out of respect for the episcopal office. As for letters such as the one to Guy of Lausanne, Bernard knew the lack of character Guy possessed yet attempted to persuade the bishop back to faithful obedience to God for the sake of his diocese.

For Bernard, the faithfulness of the bishops was reflected onto the rest of the church, as they were the examples for other ecclesiastics to follow. Their faithful lives in the midst of the many financial and worldly temptations around them offered hope to those who faced temptations in much less opulent vocations. Bernard's expectations for bishops were high, but he maintained that if they did not forget their first calling as simple priests and servants of God, they could ensure the faithfulness of the entire church.

Bishops played an important role in Bernard's ecclesiastical agenda. While he attempted to secure as many Cistercian bishops as possible, he believed that monastic affiliation alone would not suffice in restoring the church to its apostolic ideals. The individual faithfulness of the bishops would collectively foster needed spiritual reforms in the church. This could be achieved with each bishop not forgetting that beneath the flowing robes and lofty titles was a simple child of God in need of God's grace. This self-understanding would lead to obedience to Christ and faithfulness to the important office to which God had called them to serve. By attempting to direct the souls of bishops, Bernard endeavored to usher in an era of necessary change he believed the church desperately needed—a Body of Christ in which prayer, contemplation, and singularity of purpose were the motivations of those in all strata of the church, not merely in the monastic community.

CHAPTER 7

The Letters of Bernard to Popes

INTRODUCTION

In medieval Europe, one needed to take care when writing a pope. Although the spiritual fatherhood of the pope was the ecclesiastical ideal, in many ways the medieval pope served more as a temporal, rather than spiritual, authority. Information has always been equated with power, and in the heavily politicized church of the twelfth century, this was certainly the case. Since the information a pope received on a daily basis from across the landscape of the church secured his power, a pope found it dangerous not to have knowledge of a conspiracy, scandal, or coup.

While Bernard certainly understood these realities, he also had expectations for popes that were based on his own personal issues. Bernard did not naïvely hold that a pope should only concern himself with spiritual affairs; the pope had God-given authority to wield political, even military, power when necessary for the sake of the church. However, Bernard held that a pope's ultimate responsibility was the spiritual health of his children. He had a high view of the papacy and was strong supporter of the office, exhorting others to follow the pope's mandates like obedient children.[1]

As the Bride of Christ, both the earthly and the heavenly realms of the church must work together to fulfill the work entrusted to them. The

---

1. Bernard did not always find it necessary to apply this obedience to himself. For example, in *Ep* 152, he apologizes for not heeding the call of Innocent II to come to Rome, stating that he has children to nourish (*SBOp* 7:325-26). Fracheboud suggests, referring to this letter, that at times Bernard was more comfortable volunteering his assistance than heeding the request for his assistance. This is yet another example of the conflicted nature of Bernard's call. "Je Suis La Chimèra De Mon Siècle" 45–52.

role of the church on earth is to represent Christ through individual and institutional faithfulness, made possible by following the contemplative example of the angels. According to Bernard, the role of angels is to ascend to the throne of Christ through contemplation and descend to the earth out of compassion for humanity.[2] Although earthly humans cannot physically ascend to the throne of Christ, spiritual ascension is possible through mystical union with Christ, exemplified through Christ's real presence in the sacraments.[3] The implication of this ecclesiastical understanding is that if Christ's presence is in the sacraments, then salvation is possible only through humanity's participation in the church.

For Bernard the church has the ultimate authority on earth. Following the Gregorian reforms in the previous century in which the pope demonstrated the authority of the church over the state, Rome had established itself as a centralized power the secular world could not ignore. Bernard embraced this two-sword authority as a Christ-ordained role of the church in the world, although in the tradition of Gelasius I he maintained that the spiritual sword of the church was more important than the temporal sword. For example, Bernard writes to the people of Milan, reminding them to reconcile with Innocent II following the papal schism. He reminds them that although the church is merciful, it is also powerful. Bernard warns them, "You wish not to abuse her mercy or you may be crushed by her power."[4] Just as God is a benevolent Father, God is also the powerful authority in the world. The church has been given the right to exert the authority of God by virtue of its role as the holy Bride; however, those in leadership positions in the church are still under the authority of Christ, and must remember their need for humility. "Is it possible that as the Supreme Pontiff that you think you are supreme?" Bernard asks Pope Eugenius III, "Know that you are the lowest if you think you are the supreme. Who is supreme? He to whom nothing can be added."[5] As pope, Eugenius has authority in the church but not the supreme authority, which belongs to Christ alone. Everyone has a place in the ecclesiastical hierarchy, and everyone in that hierarchy, including the pope, is accountable to Christ.

Bernard's epistolary corpus contains letters to six different popes, although from the letters that survive, to three of them he wrote only once,

2. *Qui* 11.6; *SBOp* 4:452.
3. McGinn, *Growth of Mysticism*, 180.
4. *Ep* 131; *SBOp* 7:326.
5. *Csi* 2.14; *SBOp* 3:422.

and stylistically these letters are quite formal in nature. When comparing Bernard's papal letters to his letters to others in the church, his emotional style and dramatic tendencies are quite apparent, although in the letters to popes, Bernard seems to follow the *ars dictaminis* more scrupulously than he does to other letter recipients.

DE CONSIDERATIONE

Examining Bernard's letters to popes is fruitless without first understanding his ecclesiastical ideals for the papacy. The definitive document containing Bernard's papal theological construction is his *On Consideration*, written for the Cistercian Eugenius III. Like many of his works, Bernard composed this treatise in response to a request, this time from the pope himself. Eugenius, a disciple of Bernard since 1130, requested counsel from the abbot of Clairvaux as the best means to exist both as a Cistercian and as the pope—a daunting and paradoxical existence. Bernard wrote *De Consideratione* to help his spiritual son in the matters of heart and state. Written in five books, in this treatise Bernard encourages the pope to consider first himself, then what is below him, what is around him, and what is above him. The abbot begins not with God (what is above him), but with the person of Eugenius. Only after Eugenius understands himself is he able to gain control of his papal authority. Once he has dealt with his authority, then he can deal with administering and trusting those around him. Only then is he able to consider the heavenly realm, after having made peace with the first three.

Bernard's basic theme in this work is for Eugenius not to forget that despite his silken robes as Supreme Pontiff, he is still a Cistercian monk. He had not transformed from one into the other. The attitude, simplicity, and spirit that characterized his life in the cloister may be difficult to reproduce in this new role, but it is attainable. Bernard writes, "Suppose yourself as being from the substance of our origin and from the mystery of redemption, so that, seated on high, you are not highly wise, but you think humbly of yourself and be in agreement with the humble."[6] At his core, Eugenius is not a pope, but a humble child of God. Forgetting this reality would spell certain disaster for his soul. Self-knowledge as a spiritual condition was essential for a pope to have a secure, blessed papacy.

In the fourth book, Bernard offers his spiritual son counsel on how he should administer and involve himself with those in the Curia and general

6. *Csi* 2.17; *SBOp* 3:426.

administration; a bold proposition from one who had never held a title greater than abbot. In a list concluding the book, Bernard submits to Eugenius a comprehensive, scripture-laden list of both the ideals and the roles he should have as he manages his daily papal activities:

> You ought to be a model of justice, a mirror of holiness, an exemplar of piety, a preacher of truth, a defender of the faith, the teacher of the nations (1 Tim 2:7), the leader of Christians, a friend of the Bridegroom (Jn 3:29), an attendant of the bride, the director of the clergy, the shepherd of the people, the instructor of the foolish (Ro 2:20), the refuge of the oppressed, the advocate of the poor, the hope   of the unfortunate, the protector of orphans, the judge of widows (Ps 67:6), the   eye of the blind (Is 29:18), the tongue of the mute (Is 35:6), the support of the aged (Tob 25:3), the avenger of crimes, the terror of evildoers, the glory of the good, the staff of the powerful (Ps 109:2), the hammer of tyrants, the father of kings, the moderator of laws, the dispenser of canons, the salt of the earth (Mt 5:13), the light of the world (Jn 12:46), the priest of the Most High (Gen 14:18), the vicar of Christ, the anointed of the Lord (1 Sam 26:9), and finally, the god of Pharaoh (Ex 7:1).[7]

Rather than merely suggesting a comprehensive list of duties, Bernard evokes images found in Scripture, including images of Christ himself. The lesson Bernard offers Eugenius he borrows from Gregory the Great: to maintain both political and spiritual faithfulness, the pope must emulate none other than Christ, who came to serve. Bernard attempts to offer spiritual direction to the pope by reminding him of the biblical qualities Eugenius must emulate in his own life before he will be able to successfully guide the lives of others in the church.

LETTER 359 TO CALIXTUS II (1124)

Letter 359 regards the unfortunate situation with Arnold, Abbot of Morimund, who left without permission for the Holy Land with a handful of monks. This is a carefully crafted letter and formal in style. Bernard, following word he has received that Arnold was seeking papal license for his pilgrimage, encourages the pope not to give an audience to Arnold, for, as Bernard writes, "assess carefully how greatly would that occasion be a

---

7. *Csi* 4.23; *SBOp* 3:466.

destruction to our Order." If Calixtus gives countenance to Arnold, he argues, then any other Cistercian with a complaint could bypass the Order's authority and make a petition straight to Rome. Although Bernard does not explicitly tell Calixtus how to conduct business, he comes very close.[8]

As a young reformation order, Bernard believed the reputation of the Cistercians was at stake. Certainly, this crisis was an embarrassing situation that should have been handled internally. Now that Rome was involved, Bernard took it upon himself to speak on behalf of the entire Order. The Cistercians were gaining momentum with new foundations throughout the church, and the abbot was attempting to avert any public scandal that might thwart this energy. As the young abbot of Clairvaux was establishing his reformational agenda in the church, he shuddered at the thought of that agenda being impeded by a scandal in his own Order. This letter attempted to thwart any papal displeasure with the Cistercians. This issue alone secures the importance of this missive in the epistolary corpus.

However, this letter involves a more substantial issue: the proper role and procedure of accountability. In this instance, those in Cistercian leadership attempted to provide correction and direction to Arnold. As the abbot of Morimund's superiors, they had a responsibility to act in the best interests of the abbey, the Order, and Arnold himself. Although Arnold appealed to the pope, the intervention by Calixtus would undermine the authority of the Cistercian abbots. By granting Arnold's request, the pope would exceed his papal responsibilities by not conferring with the Cistercians before rendering his decision. For Bernard, this disregard of proper accountability and discipline would be inexcusable. By sharing his disregard for the pope's potential involvement in this issue, Bernard attempts to offer the pontiff a lesson in papal authority and the importance of following proper order in the church. Proper order in the church stems from proper order in the spiritual lives of those who rule the church. Fundamentally, this counsel to Calixtus regards the pope's own spiritual life, for if his life is properly ordered, he will possess the capacity to rule well and faithfully.

8. The wayward Arnold did seek an audience with Calixtus who, in turn, not only met with him but also (unfortunately for the Cistercians) gave consent for his pilgrimage to Jerusalem.

LETTER 49 TO HONORIUS II (1129)

Letter 49 was sent to the pope under under the signatures of Stephen Harding of Cîteaux, Hugh de Vitriaco of Pontigny, and Bernard. The language of the letter is clearly Bernardine, yet it demonstrates the rational influence of Stephen and Hugh.

The letter begins with an interesting statement regarding Bernard's understanding of the monastic vocation and purpose. He writes, "We who remain in our monasteries on account of our sins, pray without ceasing for you and for the church of God entrusted to you." Despite the formalities of the *ars dictaminis*, the humility with which the letter begins demonstrates the senders of the letter address their concerns for no reason other than the best interest of both the pontiff and the church. Knowing themselves to be sinners, they are shut away in their monasteries with the vocational call to pray for the church and its leaders. The inherent statement Bernard makes about the nature of the church is clear. Because the welfare of the church relies on their monastic seclusion, the issue at hand must be of the utmost importance for them to remove themselves from their cloistered interests to compose this letter. Their hope is that the pope will recognize their importance of the church and respond to their request.

The letter is written on behalf of Henry, Archbishop of Sens, who had defended the Bishop of Paris and turned the wrath of the king upon himself. In the letter, Bernard refers to the king of France as another Herod who is threatened by the Christ who reigns in the churches of France. Bernard accuses the French monarch of assailing not individuals, but religion itself. By sending this letter under three signatures instead of one, the danger of making these bold statements against their own king is abated. The reality is that medieval epistolary rhetoric was anything but secure. Although letters were sealed with the sender's imprimatur, letters were public documents. In making accusatory statements like these against one's own king, the sender of a letter could not guarantee the king would not obtain access to the letter. The threat of royal retribution against three prominent church leaders would be far more difficult than if the letter was written in the name of just one person.

This letter demonstrates the importance of the communal, rather than individual, nature of the church. While the church is comprised of many individuals, they are all part of one Christ's body. The situation in Paris affects the whole church, not just the Parisian diocese. As the shepherd of the church, the pope must act to keep this dangerous threat from infiltrating the entire flock. The three signatures on this letter demonstrates that this ecclesiological assumption represents more than just Bernard's ideology. In fact, it represents an intrinsic statement that the situation in Paris is affecting the three communities represented by the senders of the letter. No one situation or individual in the church resides in isolation. The Holy Spirit, under the stewardship of the church leadership, connects the various enterprises in the church to one another in spiritual unity and love. While political motives are surely present in this letter, these three abbots affirm the political nature of the church as a means employed by the Holy Spirit to achieve God's purposes for the church.

THE LETTERS TO INNOCENT II

Innocent II owed a considerable debt to Bernard. His disputed election, held under secrecy and out of sight of a majority of the Curia, took nearly a decade to resolve, and only then after the death of his rival, Anacletus II. Bernard's health already in question, the diligence with which Bernard endeavored for Innocent nearly exhausted him to death. The abbot traveled extensively and wrote countless letters on behalf of Innocent's claim to the papacy. For Bernard, the decision as to who was the rightful pope was simple: in his mind, Anacletus was controlled by money and power and Innocent was controlled by the power of God. Whether or not the abbot had document proof of their inner motivations was immaterial. Bernard had convinced others that Anacletus was the *bestia illa de Apocalypsi* and must be defeated.[9] Following the death of Anacletus and the stabilization of Innocent's rule, Bernard the politician knew his papal influence had never been stronger. Bernard wrote no less than fifty letters to Innocent during his pontificate, many of which were appeals for the abbot's causes or in support of his friends. In the end, Innocent became frustrated with Bernard's many appeals, and the abbot lost the favor of the pope for whom he had fought so ardently.

Letter 136 (1134)

Letter 136 is a simple letter of encouragement and petition written to Innocent during the height of the papal schism. Bernard had been working

---

9. *Ep* 125; *SBOp* 7:308.

tirelessly on Innocent's behalf and wanted to ensure the pope was remaining positive in the situation. He begins the letter by placing perspective on the papal situation: "If things were always sorrowful, who could endure it? If things were always favorable, who wouldn't take it for granted?" Bernard is encouraging Innocent to seek a balanced life that is able to endure both the times of struggle and of blessing. This example of Bernard's optimism is but one example of what drew people to him. He could be pressing, opinionated and even judgmental, but these examples of his fallen human nature actually made him more of a prophetic saint than a restless abbot in the eyes of others. He reminds Innocent in this letter that despite the struggles of his office, he is called to be obedient to Christ through the situations God has placed before him.

Obedience is a common theme throughout Bernard's works. Rightly understood by any lover of Christ, obedience in Bernard stems from desire within the obedient person, not coercion from a Master God.[10] Obedience is faithfulness to God that grows from humility. To be faithful is to understand oneself, one's place in the Kingdom of God, and one's responsibilities. For the church to be the faithful Bride of Christ, she must be faithful at all ecclesiastical strata. Bernard's understanding of obedience involves a synergy between direct and mediated obedience, for one is faithful to God and to the church at once.

Bernard had high ideals for everyone, and, at times, the abbot could be accused of naïvely believing that others shared his ideals. His Rule for the Knights Templar, for example, is filled with statements of monastic bliss that secular knights could not be expected to maintain. According to Bernard, the disobedient attitude of pride, particularly among those in leadership in the institutional church, is a grave sin, and ambition should have no place in the Body of Christ.[11] For Bernard, both the pope and a monk should have the same understanding of faithfulness to Christ through humility. Because the saint believed the church to exist in both heaven and on earth, he argued the perfect monk was very much like an angel, in that God charges them both to act out of charity alone.[12] A life of charity is a life following the example of Christ, who lovingly shines his light into Christians that they might impart it to others.[13] The church is faithful when

---

10. Gilson, *Mystical Theology of St. Bernard*, 111.

11. Bernard calls ambition in the church *insipientia* and a *virus*. *Csi* 3.5; *SBOp* 3:434.

12. *Qui* 11.11; *SBOp* 4:456.

13. *Asc* 4.2; *SBOp* 5:138.

the individuals within the church live faithfully to their vocational calling. This understanding of faithfulness and obedience, rather than self-service and ambition, is what enabled Bernard to support Innocent over Anacletus.

LETTER 213 (1139)

Letter 213 is an important letter regarding an event in the aftermath of the papal schism. Cardinal Priest Peter of Pisa, who had formerly supported Anacletus, was reconciled to Innocent in the midst of the schism through the direct involvement of Bernard of Clairvaux. This reunion was a considerable achievement for the abbot of Clairvaux. Nevertheless, shortly after the resolution of the schism, Innocent deprived of office all supporters and former supporters of the antipope. Bernard responded to Innocent with this letter, which many believe resulted in Innocent turning his back on Bernard.

Bernard begins the letter with a bold statement: "If I had a judge before whom I could drag you, I would soon show you . . . what you deserve." He states he wishes he could summon Innocent before the tribunal of Christ, but since he cannot, he will arraign him before himself. Bernard warns that by punishing Peter of Pisa, with whom he had been reconciled through Bernard's intervention, Innocent was guilty of condemning Bernard as a traitor against both Innocent himself and the church.

What follows is nothing less than a cross-examination of Innocent, with Bernard citing evidence and then rhetorically asking the pope to disprove it. He asks, "Can it be that you did not appoint me as your representative for the reconciliation of Peter of Pisa?. . . If you deny it, I can prove it by as many witnesses as there were men in the Curia at that time." Bernard continues the strong cross-examination with further questions about the pope's inconsistent behavior.

Bernard concludes the letter with a sardonic statement from one who knows he has been deceived. He writes, "I have written to you another time on this matter, but because I had not received an answer, I suppose what I had written did not reach you." Bernard knew that Innocent had received his previous letter; however, this cynical conclusion indicates Bernard knew his close relationship with Innocent was over. This closing line was Bernard's attempt to appear naïve, but with the knowledge that Innocent knew that he was anything but naïve. Despite this letter's emotional character, it demonstrates Bernard's belief that the pope was not being faithful to his call as the bishop of Rome. He had forgotten that he serves Almighty God.

The classification of authority was part of Bernard's culture, so the process of presenting God as the ultimate authority in both heaven and on earth was not difficult to construct. Although earthly authorities rule by virtue of their placement in society, Bernard describes God's authority as stemming from his divine nature and being evident through God's creative works. While humanity and the angels have only one excellence, the ability to reason, God's excellence is not limited to reason; rather, God is wholly and completely excellent and thus has a complete capacity for reason.[14]

In this letter, Bernard reminds Innocent that he is in his position not by his own power, but by God's grace.[15] Although he is the pope, he is a steward of God who placed him in that position. Unless he has a healthy understanding of himself and his role, he will not serve God faithfully but will rule with a false understanding of himself, which is pride. In *The Steps of Humility and Pride*, Bernard writes, "If a man wants to understand the full truth about himself, he will have to remove the timber of pride that blocks the light from his eye and set up a set of stairs in his heart so that he can examine himself."[16] Thus, for Bernard, acknowledging the absolute authority of God begins by first having a healthy understanding of oneself, as one sees the need for divine mercy and grace, which naturally leads to a life of humility. Without humility, one cannot attain a proper view of God. God is the Creator, while humanity the created. Humility of heart allows the Christian to have a full understanding of this statement: As created beings, all persons are equally under the authority of God the Father, regardless of their position or title on earth.

LETTER 218 (1143)

Letter 218 relates to *Letter 213* in that Bernard seems to have forgotten the harsh and discourteous language of the previous letter. In *Letter 218*, the abbot seems confused that Innocent has not written to him in some time. He begins the letter as an abandoned child, bemoaning the fact that he used to think that he had a place of small importance in Innocent's life, but now he is reduced to nothing. Innocent used to hear Bernard's requests and

14. *Csi* 5.5; *SBOp* 3:470.

15. For other examples of this language, see *Epp* 29, 64, 139, 158, 309, 497.

16. *Hum* 15; *SBOp* 3:27.

return his letters, but now Innocent has averted his face from him. Bernard asks, "But why? What mistake did I make?" He cites several possible reasons, but remains puzzled that Innocent would disregard his influence. These two questions involve three possible scenarios: either Bernard truly did not understand what he had done, he did not want to admit his own mistakes, or he wanted to appear naïve to Innocent. If Bernard did not understand his faults, then he did not have a healthy understanding of himself or his motivations. If he did not want to admit the erroneous tone in his previous letters, then he was demonstrating pride. If he was attempting to manipulate the pope, he was avoiding confessing his errors. Any of these scenarios shows Bernard negatively. He found himself in disfavor with the very pope he championed for nearly a decade through over-ambition and not knowing when to restrain himself from going beyond the limits of acceptable epistolary behavior.

LETTER 358 TO CELESTINE II (1143)

This eight sentence, fourteen-line letter was written on behalf of Bernard's friend and patron, Count Theobald "the Great" of Champagne, who had made a request to the pope regarding a particular situation that he believed would bring stability to the region. In his text, Bernard uses the word "peace" (*pacis/pacem*) eight times. He calls Count Theobald a "son of peace," says that he has a "zeal for peace," and that Celestine's rule is an "apostolate of peace." Since Theobald desires peace, Celestine should extend it to him. Bernard writes that Celestine has an obligation to fulfill Theobald's request, for as a friend of the Bridegroom, he should not sadden the Bride, but rather provide peace for the Bride.

For Bernard, a desire for peace with others is a demonstration of humility.[17] Peace with God cannot be achieved unless one has achieved peace in one's own life, for unless a person has so humbled his or her own heart to accept whatever God gives in life, that person cannot be at peace with God.[18] If love is a dish filled with excellent food, peace is surely on it, as is patience, kindness, longsuffering, and joy in the Holy Spirit.[19] These items of spiritual food work together to nourish us in our faithfulness to Christ. Bernard desires that Celestine's papacy be one of political peace that begins

17. *SC* 29.4; *SBOp* 1:205.
18. *SC* 13.4; *SBOp* 1:71.
19. *Hum* 4; *SBOp* 3:19.

with an inner peace in the pope's own life. He used Theobald as an example of a person in political power who possesses the ideals of this peace. That Bernard would use a secular leader as a spiritual example for a pope is quite significant in understanding the abbot's anthropology. All people, including laity, and regardless of vocation, have the capacity to live a life of faithfulness and obedience to Christ. Theobald's contribution to the church was his desire for political stability and peace, which was necessary for the work of Christ in the world.

However, rather than ending the letter focusing on the spiritual maxims of peace, Bernard reminds the pope that the pontiff should understand Bernard as the one with the spiritual authority, for he closes the letter with the words *Satis pro imperio* ("This is as much as a command"). If the pope desires to be a pontiff with a reputation of acting as a harbinger of peace, he must first understand that Bernard of Clairvaux is the means that will ensure a peaceful papal reign. Bernard's counsel to the pope is to remind him of his responsibility to serve as a shepherd to all in the church, not just those whom the pope believes has a direct relationship with him. The political affairs of Theobald, a sheep in the pope's flock, are the pope's spiritual responsibility.

LETTER 525 TO LUCIUS II (1142)

No letter from Bernard to Pope Lucius II has survived. However, before Lucius became Pope, he was Gerard Caccianemici, a Cardinal Priest and Chancellor of the Holy See. In Bernard's only letter to him, *Letter 525*, he writes on behalf of the letter bearers who had journeyed to Rome. In a closing section of the letter, Bernard warns the powerful Chancellor to ensure that as the growth of his chancellery increases, so will his charity and mercy. He warns Gerard about the shameful activity of priests of God to manage to take money from the church's moneyboxes.

Bernard closes the letter by stating while he is worried for Gerard, "I wish that you were equally worried for yourself." Beneath this statement lies a clear disdain for this powerful cardinal, who seemed to be more concerned with political aspirations than self-care and his vocational calling. As a Cardinal Priest and Chancellor, Gerard should seek for himself what God seeks for him, regardless of political situation or vocation. To seek what is not God's will is a disdain for God's love. Of course, the very fact that Bernard makes this comment to the future pope, Bernard reveals that he believes he understands Gerard and his desires better than Gerard himself.

THE LETTERS TO EUGENIUS III

Certainly one must empathize with Eugenius III (1145–1153). He spent most of his pontificate exiled from Rome, due in large part to Arnold of Brescia, the instigator against the church's temporal power, who continued to have influence over the Roman public. Eugenius was the pope of the Second Crusade, which attempted to recapture Edessa from the Muslims, but ultimately ended in disaster. While Eugenius certainly had these and other difficulties to manage as pope, he also had to cope with papal life as a former monk of Bernard of Clairvaux, who always stood ready to offer counsel, direction, and at times, scorn. Although Bernard's former monk had now assumed the papacy, Bernard was not about to cease the process of directing the pope's soul. Many of these letters to Eugenius portray Bernard negatively, as he realizes the power he holds as the spiritual father of the pope; an existing relationship he does not let Eugenius forget.

LETTER 238 (1145)

Letter 238 is perhaps the first letter written by Bernard to his former disciple following his elevation to the papacy. He begins the letter with a strong congratulatory tone: "What the Lord has brought about in your life has been heard and celebrated through the conversations of all the people." He apologizes for not writing sooner, but confesses he has been pondering this situation for some time. Bernard writes that Eugenius used to be his son, but now he is Bernard's father. Although the former monk Bernardo is now Pope Eugenius III, the new pontiff should remember he has grown in his faith because of Bernard's influence. In fact, Bernard goes so far as to assert that Eugenius owes Bernard his salvation: "If you are considered worthy [for this position], in a certain way I brought forth the gospel in you." Bernard does not want Eugenius to forget the salvific debt he owes Bernard, or the source of his spiritual growth. Bernard seems to be carefully placing himself in a needed role in the life of this new pope.

While Bernard shares that the Cistercian community throughout the church rejoices in Eugenius' ascent to the papacy, he is concerned for him. He writes that when Bernardo Paganelli became a Cistercian, he chose the *novissimo loco in convivio eius* ("the seat of least honor at God's banquet table"). Now, he writes, "Obviously, you have been assigned to a high seat, but not a safe one; an eminent one, but not a secure one. Absolutely terrible, how terrible is the seat you hold." Bernard has gone from rejoicing for Eugenius' ascension and the blessing it will bring to the church to absolute fear and terror for his soul.

The letter concludes with Bernard's famous call for reform that clearly demonstrates his conservative ecclesiology and his yearning for the glorious days of the church Fathers: "Who will grant me before I die to see the church of God as she was in the days of old: when the apostles extended their nets to catch not silver or gold, but to capture the souls of people?" He calls for Eugenius to be the leader who will actualize this vision. He exhorts Eugenius to have courage and be valiant, and to remember his enemies' necks are in his hand. The apparent contradiction between saving people's souls with the net of the church and squeezing his enemies' necks with his hand is not paradoxical for Bernard, for these are two primary responsibilities Eugenius possesses. The Apostles and church Fathers, concerned not with monetary gain, had no political might to crush their enemies. They could only cast spiritual nets. Now that the church had adequate financial resources, Bernard sees his contemporary church as being concerned primarily with political and financial gain rather than striving to be the faithful Bride of Christ.

In Bernard's mind, with his help Eugenius can finally be a pope who, after several centuries, will administer the Keys of the Kingdom faithfully. Bernard calls for a Eugenius to be a balanced papal leader who can return the church to its faithful existence under Peter and the apostles. In his many travels and interventions, Bernard had seen the corruption of the church. Now that a Cistercian was at its head, he believed the potential for extensive reform was finally attainable, and the earthly and heavenly church would be united. The two will no longer be separated by the sin of humanity, for the earthly bride has been ransomed and redeemed by the Bridegroom. Christ has mysteriously sealed the relationship between heaven and earth, and has fused the relationship between humanity and angels. The result is that upon their earthly death, the souls of the redeemed are able to join the angels as part of the heavenly Bride.[20] Although previous popes had not placed a priority on uniting the heavenly and earthly church, as a Cistercian

---

20. This idea is developed most clearly in *Sermon 27* on the *Song of Songs*.

and Bernard's spiritual son, Eugenius had an opportunity to realize this ecclesiastical ideal.

<h2 style="text-align:center">LETTER 239 (1145)</h2>

Letter 239 to Eugenius is a wonderful example of the paradox within Bernard of Clairvaux, demonstrating his insatiable interest in the affairs outside of his monastery while seeming to loathe the attention and popularity that follows. Rather than acting as an unhealthy conflict within him (or not fully understanding himself or his vocational call), this inner contention between solitude and action actually served to provide an internal balance. Due to his complete assurance of his vocation, Bernard was able to desire both action and solitude simultaneously. The two may collide from time to time but, as this letter demonstrates, they are both innate in his being.

Bernard begins *Letter 239* lamenting the attention he has received since Eugenius became pope. "I am annoyed, but I have an excuse: the apostolate of Eugenius excuses me. They say it is not you that is pope, but me, and from everywhere they flock to me with their business." Bernard states that it would be a sin for him not to help these petitioners. Although these people and their issues exasperate him and keep him from solitude with God, the abbot's empathy for them moves him to support their many causes. Implicit in these remarks, however, is an inner delight of his position (in his mind) of serving as a "shadow pope," who is the real decision-maker in the church.

However, Bernard discloses the primary reason for his letter is to support a cause that is *honestissima*: the deposition the Archbishop of York, whom Bernard calls *idolum illud Eboracense* ("that idol from York"). This event was initiated when a non-Cistercian and rather contemptuous man, William Fitzherbert, was consecrated in York. Bernard refuses to abandon his passionate intention of seeing Fitzherbert removed from office. "This is my request. This is our plea. This is the desire of our soul." This statement is certainly hyperbolic, but Bernard's emotionalism is intended on procuring the attention of the Cistercian pontiff by reminding him of his former abbot's wisdom and power. Bernard was still the director of Eugenius' soul and the one who had birthed him in the faith. For Eugenius to navigate his way through the myriad of papal responsibilities successfully, he must heed the counsel of his spiritual parent, who has Eugenius' best interest in mind.

Not only does Bernard petition that William Fitzherbert be deposed, he also asks that Eugenius support the Archbishop of Canterbury, not only for his devout life, but also "on account of my love [for him]." He concludes with an imperative for Eugenius not to put off the matter for another day. In an attempt to make the supreme pontiff accountable to him, Bernard write imperatively, "Show us what you are doing about it and tell us what you want us to do." Having one's spiritual disciple as pope has its advantages, and Bernard ventures to gain from every possible occasion. He certainly does not want to lose this opportunity to have the Archbishop of York deposed; a goal he has endeavored to accomplish for several years.[21] Bernard's desires certainly seem suspicious. It appears that his desire to offer spiritual guidance to Eugenius is for nothing more than the accomplishment of his own political agendas. At this point, it seems clear that Bernard's ability to offer spiritual direction to Eugenius has ceased to exist, for he has not humbled himself in the same manner he has asked Eugenius to do. His agenda is not Eugenius' soul, but his own political activities. Due to the success Bernard has enjoyed in his prior activities outside of Clairvaux, selfishness, rather than selflessness, has overtaken Bernard's relationship with Eugenius.

Letter 269 (1149–1152)

In this brief, angry letter, beginning with the line, *Serpens decepit me*, Bernard expresses his frustration and enmity toward an individual who gained access to one of Bernard's letters of recommendation for his own use. The language Bernard uses to describe this individual demonstrates the abbot's creative, emotional rhetorical gifts. Besides referring to this person as a serpent, he also calls him a "double faced, cunning man," an "enemy of his own conscience," a "cunning deceiver," an "evil swindler," and a "greedy oppressor." One can empathize with Bernard, for his reputation was at stake; however, he surely must have considered the possibility that given the large number of recommendations and petitions he made for countless individuals, eventually one or more of his letters would be misused.

---

21. As a result of Bernard's impassioned efforts, Eugenius III suspended Fitzherbert. After his followers (perhaps instigated by King Stephen of England) violently raided the Cistercian abbey of Fountains, Eugenius deposed Fitzherbert and ordered another election. The Cistercian Henry Murdac was elected but was not fully recognized by either the clergy or the king until six years later.

This letter serves as one of the few letters Bernard wrote on behalf of himself to help restore the potential distortion of his reputation.[22] Bernard's alarm at the potential defacement of his reputation seems to be at odds with his spiritual writings that stress the importance of knowing and being faithful to oneself. In defending his character so arduously, Bernard seems to be descending his own steps of humility and ascending the steps of pride. In *On Loving God*, Bernard writes, "To lose yourself, as if you no longer existed, to cease experiencing yourself, to reduce yourself to near destruction, is a divine experience, not a human emotion."[23] Certainly defending one's own interests is not total abandonment to God, for in reducing oneself to the extent that the self is lost in abandonment to God, then others' opinions should not matter.

At this point, a potentially disturbing portrait of Bernard emerges. It appears Bernard has divided his spiritual and political existences, creating the appearance of two separate Bernards. Had these self-defending instances occurred more regularly than they do in the epistolary corpus, one could make such an argument. However, the small percentage of these letters that exist demonstrates that this egocentricity was not commonplace. A vast majority of Bernard's letters are concerned with the health and welfare of the church. In addition, that most of these letters were in the edition established by Geoffrey of Auxerre after Bernard's death indicates, at least for Geoffrey, that these letters did not seem to threaten the anticipated canonization of the abbot.

LETTER 305 (1150)

Letter 305 is an interesting letter, demonstrating the extent to which Bernard interfered with Eugenius' administration of the papacy. Rather than attempting to control Eugenius covertly, Bernard is forthright about his actions, yet sees nothing irregular about them. Sometime around the year 1150, Eugenius had summoned Henry, Bishop of Beauvais. On his way to appear before Eugenius, Henry stopped at Clairvaux. Bernard, curious as to why Eugenius would have need of the bishop, prevented him from

---

22. Although letters written on behalf of himself (or in defense of himself) are rare, examples include, *Ep* 48; *SBOp* 7:137–140, *Ep* 218; *SBOp* 8:78–79, *Ep* 223; *SBOp* 8:89–90, and *Ep* 401; *SBOp* 8:381.

23. *Dil* 27; *SBOp* 3:142.

continuing on his journey. *Letter 305* is Bernard's explanation to the pope as to why the bishop had not yet arrived.

Although the bishop was greatly displeased at Bernard hindering his progress toward his audience with the pope, the abbot felt compelled to keep him at Clairvaux, stating to Eugenius, "We were uncertain of your purpose for him." Bernard proceeds to offer additional reasons for keeping Bishop Henry from traveling to Rome. He states in addition to the other misfortunes that appeared to impede his journey, Henry and his brother, King Louis VII of France, were not *in uno spiritu*, making it dangerous for Henry to be away from his country. Although it was the bishop whom Eugenius sought, Bernard has sent one of his assistants instead, which is far better for the church in France than if the bishop were to have gone himself.

Other than Bernard's disregard of Eugenius' geopolitical limits of recruitment for the Second Crusade, his conspicuous doubt of Eugenius' judgment in this letter demonstrates the abbot's growing boldness in the administration of ecclesiastical affairs. Not only did Eugenius have to deal with the growing political tensions in Rome, his exile in France, the pending news of the Second Crusade, and the general management of the church, he also faced defiance from his spiritual father and perhaps the most respected person in Europe.

This letter demonstrates that although Bernard often wrote of the authority of Rome, he took advantage of his relationship with Eugenius and disregarded his place in the church as the abbot of Clairvaux. Rather than withdrawing from worldly affairs, he usurps the will of the pope to achieve his own agenda. In this situation, he seems to be at odds with his own ecclesiology and perception of the church.

CONCLUSIONS

In Bernard's mind, a pope's function in the church was to serve as the successor of Peter, who was foremost a follower of Christ. While his authority was God-given, it was not absolute. Because his position was God-ordained, he must be shown appropriate respect. However, beneath his silken robes a pope was a man in need of divine grace like everyone else in the church. Certainly the pope had a role in the Kingdom of God, as did bishops, priests, monks, and laypersons. Yet as the head of the church, the church's health depended upon his faithfulness to Christ and personal sanctity.

It must be noted that in many of his papal letters, Bernard appears to be lacking in the proper respect of his pontiff. He instructs the pope how he should rule, attempts manipulation, and in other instances even thwarts direct orders or desires of the pope. He appears rather arrogant at times and proud of his position in the church. Nevertheless, Bernard's tone in these letters can be interpreted not as arrogance, but rather absolute confidence in his vocation and calling. Bernard understood himself to such an extent that he believed without any doubt that his placement in the church at this point in history was divinely ordained. The abbot of Clairvaux did not hesitate offering this counsel to popes, for he felt that he had spiritual wisdom to impart to them. While it seems that Bernard's letters to popes are nothing more than advancing his own agenda, it is quite plausible that what appears to be manipulation and selfishness could have been in Bernard's mind sincere spiritual counsel. Bernard's confidence in his abilities and vocation were unshakable. He knew that people respected his counsel and spiritual insights.

To be sure, his expectations for papal leaders were exceedingly high, but they were no higher than the spiritual and political expectations he placed upon himself. We have already noted that for Bernard, if any issue in the church concerned Christ, it concerned him. In many ways Bernard had placed himself in the role as the protector and shepherd of the church—a role reserved for the popes. Bernard understood his role, however, as the abbot of the church. Although a papal function, this vocational understanding enabled him to be unaccountable to others. Bernard never held an official title higher than that of Abbot of Clairvaux, yet his activities greatly exceeded that designation.

Can Bernard be accused of arrogance and opportunism? Some have made this claim.[24] Judging Bernard too quickly, however, and through a modern historical lens, is to view him unfairly. The abbot of Clairvaux's sole desire was the restoration of the church through the reformation of each person in the church. To be sure, it was his own interpretation of how the church should be reformed and how it should operate, but unlike others in his generation, his own interests were not at the forefront of his activities, despite any contrary appearances. His confidence as the hand of God in the church compelled him towards reform for both within and outside of monasticism. As we have noted, not all appreciated or accepted this

24. Bredero, *Bernard of Clairvaux*; Diers, *Bernhard von Clairvaux*.

confidence. Bernard was indeed a saint, but he was a saint whose humanity at times interfered with his holy aspirations.

CHAPTER 8

The Letters of Bernard to Laity

INTRODUCTION

THE TERM "LAITY" ENCOMPASSES a wide range of groups. A medieval layperson could be a king, a member of the nobility, someone in the middle class, or a peasant. That Bernard either wrote to or on behalf of individuals in each of these groups demonstrates the comprehensiveness of his interests. Rather than understanding the Kingdom of God as an entity reserved for clerics and the matters of Rome, Bernard presumed that the church encompassed all persons, regardless of stature or position. Every living soul had a place in the church. While the monastic community sought obedience to Christ by following the *Rule* of Benedict, the laity, according to Bernard, also followed a Rule a rule as well: the Ten Commandments.[1]

Bernard wrote more than seventy-five letters to laypersons, including nearly thirty letters to kings and emperors. The content of these letters varies, but most include Bernard's political views on a number of issues, and many include spiritual counsel or warnings of some sort. No less than twenty letters are addressed to counts or countesses, several of which, such as Count Theobald of Champagne, were Cistercian benefactors.

These letters demonstrate Bernard's ability to participate in the political arena with all appropriateness necessary to impress and influence those in power. Yet despite the political overtones in many of these letters, Bernard was able to accomplish this without compromising his ecclesiastical reforming mission. At times Bernard was surprisingly bold to members of the nobility, deriding them at times for their lack of faith or support of

---

1. *Div* 9.3; *SBOp* 6/1:119.

his own causes, even when the "cause" seemed trivial or beyond his responsibilities.[2] Despite these indiscretions, his fundamental concern for these secular leaders remained their relationship with Christ. Bernard understood that the temporal power these nobles possessed meant that few people dared to speak plainly to them about issues in their personal lives. Bernard displayed no such fear, for in writing with the authority of God, his concern was directing their souls. Rather than focusing on groups of laity in his letters, he stressed the importance of the individual soul. In fact, the emphasis that Bernard placed on the individual cannot be stressed enough. Indeed, to fully grasp Bernard's spirituality, one could argue that he was a twelfth-century humanist, interested in the inner workings of what makes the individual fully human and fully God's.

Bernard wrote fewer than thirty letters to ordinary laypersons (not including the secular nobility). Not surprisingly, a majority of these letters concerned personal spiritual matters rather than the affairs of ecclesiastical politics. Bernard was careful to leave the dealings of the church with those who have control to enact reform. To common laypersons, Bernard wrote primarily about their spiritual commitments and discipline, including chastisement for not fulfilling a monastic promise. A few of the letters were written to parents of sons who entered the Cistercian Order, either to console them in the loss of their sons or condemn them for interfering in their son's call to the monastic life.

Following the model of Gregory the Great, who believed that all Christians can attain an ascetic lifestyle,[3] Bernard had high expectations for the spiritual development of the laity. Bernard's letters to laypersons can be categorized in a number of ways. This chapter focuses specifically on his letters to royalty, noblemen, young men (particularly those who had made a monastic intention), married couples, and certain laypersons who bear significance.

Quite clear in Bernard's letters is the idea that, while the monastic life (particularly the Cistercian life) is the surest way to faithfulness to God, all Christians—from the pope to the peasant—have an important role in the life of the church on earth. For example, Bernard begins *Letter 497* to Count Theobald of Champagne with the salutation, "To Count Theobald,

2. For example, in a letter to Count Henry, son of Theobald, Bernard gives a strong warning from God if Henry does not replace the pigs lost by one of his peasants. *Ep 279*; *SBOp* 8:191. Other examples of letters in this genre are *Ep 97*; *SBOp* 7:247–48 and *Ep 128*; *SBOp* 7:321–22.

3. Demacopoulos, *Five Models of Spiritual Direction in the Early Church*, 163.

whom I believe to be a faithful minister of God." While true that Bernard relied upon Theobald's financial generosity and political support, the abbot would not have used such language had he not truly believed it. For example, Bernard did not have the affection or trust of Theobald's son, Henry, who succeeded his father; an opinion the abbot did not keep to himself. Another example is *Letter 289* to Queen Melisande of Jerusalem, in which Bernard writes that he has heard evil reports about her.

Thematically, these letters reflect the whole of Bernard's epistolary corpus. Through them, the abbot attempts to re-focus the attention of the laity from personal fulfillment to selflessness. He exhorts them to seek humility rather than human accolades. He stresses the need for the church and the state to work in divine harmony. Above all, he reminds the laity that they are called to first serve Christ through obedience to Christ's church on earth.

LETTERS TO MEMBERS OF THE ROYALTY

The importance of kings to monks was substantial. Not only did they at times allocate royal lands for monastic purposes, they also installed bishops who would rule over the monasteries in their dioceses. Becoming embroiled in the matters of state required careful maneuvering, for upsetting the royalty could have disastrous effects, as in the case of Stephen of Senlis, the Bishop of Paris, who in the mid-1120s upset King Louis VI by initiating reforms that were unfavorable to the king. Bernard writes to the nobility with the voice of a respectful prophet, akin more to Isaiah than to Jeremiah.[4]

LETTER 255 TO KING LOUIS VI OF FRANCE (1135)

Letter 255 serves as a good example of Bernard's letters to the nobility. He begins the letter with a formal salutation to the "Most excellent King of France." However, Bernard reminds Louis he is writing on behalf of "The King of Kings and Lord of Lords." This statement, albeit in the salutation of the letter, serves as a spiritual lesson to the king that he is not the ultimate authority in France. Since secular authorities understood their reigns as

---

4. Sommerfeldt, suggests that for Bernard the state was as much a religious institution as was the institutional church. "Vassals of the Lord and Ministers of God," 56.

competing with various jurisdictions, feudatories, and even the church, Bernard's salutation could not have been seen potentially as a competition for Louis' jurisdiction. This seemingly unimportant *salutatio* is Bernard's means of obtaining the king's attention by alluding that although the text that follows in the letter is from Bernard of Clairvaux, its authority originates with Almighty God. To be a faithful king, Louis should understand himself and his role in relationship to God's view of Louis and God's purposes for his life.

The letter regards Pope Innocent II's circulation of a bull calling forth a Council at Pisa at Pentecost in 1135. Since the papal schism was not yet resolved, Louis (and to a lesser extent his advisor Suger) seemed uninterested in the Council and forbade French clergy from attending. Innocent believed the council would further legitimize his papacy. The council would deal with issues of simony, discipline, and the excommunication of Roger of Sicily and Anacletus for a second time. Attending the council was explicit support for Innocent II's papal authority. Since medieval kings never knew how long their reigns would endure, this public support for Innocent was something Louis wished to avoid.

Bernard begins the letter by asking the king a very pointed rhetorical question: "Why, my lord, are you angry and enraged against the elected one of God, whom your highness has also received and chosen beforehand as a father for yourself, and even a Samuel for your son?" This straightforward approach is an attempt for the king to know how disturbed Bernard is by the king's actions against Innocent II. In the past, Louis supported Innocent throughout the papal schism. Bernard cannot understand why the French king would suddenly turn on the pontiff. Perhaps Bernard cannot comprehend the idea that King Louis could support the pope without supporting all of the pope's actions. For Bernard, Louis either supports the pope or condemns him. He leaves no latitude for anything in between the two extremes. He chides the king for a lack of forthrightness in support of Innocent, suggesting that the king lacks political courage and trust in God.

The abbot concludes this letter by stating that his desire is what is in the king's best interest. For example, if the king has troubles with the issues set forth in this Council, the most effective way to resolve the issues is to send for the French bishops and let them argue in favor of the king's position. Not having French representation would be more damaging to Louis' reign than his public support of Innocent. Whether or not Louis had the discernment to realize Bernard's manipulative strategy is difficult to discern, but the result of this letter is that the king relented, and following Bernard's counsel rather than Suger's, allowed the French clergy to travel to Pisa.

Through this letter, Bernard successfully transformed a political skirmish into a spiritual lesson of obedience to God. Bernard reminded the king that spirituality exists in all areas of one's life, not merely while celebrating the Mass. Every decision Louis makes will have a direct influence on his relationship with Christ. In order for the king to rule well, he must understand that his reign is subservient to the reign of Christ, and that as ruler of France, he must first allow Christ to rule his life.

LETTER 449 TO KING LOUIS VII OF FRANCE (1139–1140)

The pious son of King Louis VI, Louis VII was raised to follow an ecclesiastical career. Following the unexpected death of his brother Philip in 1131, he became the reluctant King of France in 1137. Louis was a scholarly man who seemed to have preferred the life of a priest to the life of a king. In fact, Walter Map wrote that Louis VII, while adept at the martial arts, was in other respects little more than an imbecile."[5] As the first husband of the enterprising and ambitious Eleanor of Aquitaine, Louis' attention to the matters of God instead of the matters of marriage became a constant frustration to his queen. Fifteen years after their marriage in 1137, Eleanor had the marriage dissolved on the grounds of consanguinity.

When Bernard was offered Archbishop of Rheims in 1139, he flatly refused the appointment. *Letter 449* is written to Louis VII to express his regret at having been named for this See. The letter begins with Bernard expressing his devotion to Louis and conveying that he knows Louis has nothing but the best of intentions. He knows that Louis would never have promoted such a *miseri hominus* for such a lofty position except for the cause of God. He complains not only did Louis consent to his election; he requested the Bernard accept it. Bernard states that although Louis has promised his support and protection of Bernard in Rheims, Bernard questions Louis' effectiveness in being able to accomplish this feat. In a statement lacking subtlety, Bernard replies condescendingly, "This could only come from a royal king with childish maturity!"

Bernard continues by lamenting his broken body and his insignificant persona. He compares himself to Job, stating all that remains for him is the

5. Warren, *Henry II*, 20.

grave. For the king to ask Bernard to leave his sons at Clairvaux would be sinful and cruel and would "not promote prayers, but weeping." Bernard's stylistically driven humility may have been a rhetorical device, but it serves as an effective means of making his argument perfectly clear to the king: The only title he should ever hold is that of Abbot of Clairvaux. Although Bernard has ideas about what the archbishopric of Rheims needs, he does not desire the responsibility that comes with an episcopal appointment. While it was true that Bernard did not want to leave Clairvaux for the sake of his monks, his refusal cannot be seen as noble, for in other situations Bernard has encouraged those elected to the bishopric to see this as the movement of God. In this situation, the abbot of Clairvaux has separated himself from the standards of others, which is hardly a noble or virtuous attitude. Bernard seems to thrive on the outside, offering advice and counsel without accountability. Had he accepted the archbishopric, he would be politically and spiritually responsible for the bodies and souls of those in the region. He found it much easier to offer counsel without having to endure the personal consequences and accountability from his counsel.

Although this characterization of Bernard is somewhat questionable, his refusal of this appointment is squarely in line with his vocational withdrawal from the world. The riches and power of a medieval archbishop would have changed Bernard's life dramatically and served as a total reversal from the Cistercian ideal of fleeing from the world. In fact, his frail body would not have been able to withstand the anxiety of such a position. Bernard's confidence in his divine calling permitted him to withstand accepting this position, a request he perceived to be a temptation, not an opportunity. The lesson to Louis VII is that he should never ask Bernard to do anything that would deviate from Bernard's vocational call. The attitude of pride intrinsic in this message to the French king views Bernard quite negatively. It is difficult to conceive of the young Bernard who wrote *The Steps of Humility and Pride* twenty years earlier making statements similar to those in this letter. The middle-aged Bernard had gained confidence in his political acumen, and despite his attempts to restore the church to the glory of its past, he was contributing to its current state of selfish individualism. To be sure, Bernard believed his actions were divinely inspired. However, his spiritual elitism portrays him negatively from time to time.

The primary, implicit spiritual lesson to Louis VII is that one needs to be confident in the role God has assigned him or her in the world. The French king seemed uncomfortable administering his kingdom. His interests were spiritual, not political, and he found himself thrust into a life in two worlds: the spiritual and the political. By refusing this espiscopal appointment, Bernard was offering an implicit spiritual lesson to Louis: God had assigned him a kingly role, not a monastic one, in this life. Faithfulness to Christ in his life would be manifest by serving as a king that stood for justice and godliness.

Letter 221 to King Louis VII of France (1143)

Although Louis VII was known for his piety, at times he displayed cruelty and harsh retribution toward his enemies. When Louis refused to acknowledge the election of the archbishop of Bourges, his two-year war with Count Theobald II of Champagne came to a violent climax, when in 1143 King Louis laid waste to the Champagne countryside and burned to the ground the town of Vitry. More than fifteen hundred people, hundreds of whom sought refuge in the town church, were burned to death in the slaughter. Louis sent Bernard a letter, making excuses for his actions. The abbot of Clairvaux responded with *Letter 221*, which demonstrates many of the abbot's recurring epistolary themes.

Citing Psalm 140:4, Bernard chastises Louis for attempting to make excuses in his sins. Louis has not sought sound advice before and during the entire Champagne campaign. The abbot asks, "From whom but the devil could the counsel come that results in what you are doing? It is becoming fire upon fire, murder upon murder, and the voice of the poor, the groans of the captives, and the blood of those murdered echoes in the ears of the Father of orphans and the Judge of widow." Bernard writes his love for Louis had been so strong, and his trust of the king's judgment had been so great that he had written letters to the pope supporting the young king. Now, based upon the burning of Vitry and the murder of nearly everyone in the town, Bernard has regrets for having supported Louis and is determined to expose the truth about Louis' actions.

Bernard closes the letter expressing fear for Louis' soul. He writes he has been harsh to the young king because he fears what Louis will face in the life to come because of what he has done. He encourages Louis to seek humility and do penance before the vengeance of God strikes him. The harsh exhortation may have been successful, for less than two years later, the emotional and superstitious Louis, still stricken with grief over his actions at Vitry and his subsequent papal excommunication, completed his penance by funding and leading the Second Crusade.

This letter raises the issue of justice as a natural progression of self-knowledge. By destroying the village of Vitry, Louis was acting not in his God-assigned role as a secular ruler, but out of his own misunderstanding of himself. Peace and justice are the responsibility of the secular rulers. When their actions result in contrary results, they are clearly demonstrating their lack of self-understanding. Because Louis did not have a healthy understanding of himself or his role as king, he blurred the distinction between the roles of church and state, resulting in a murderous situation.

Personal ambition, rather than kingly justice, was the root of the French king expressing his anger against Theobald through the destruction of Vitry. Had Louis not succumbed to the temptation of pride, this massacre would never have occurred. Rather than submitting to the pope's decision to name the archbishop of Bourges, Louis determined to assert his authority over France by warring with Theobald, who supported the pope's episcopal choice. Until Louis was willing to submit himself before God and the pope, he would be disconnected from divine fellowship. Only when the king prevailed in placing his rule under the authority of Christ would he stand faithfully in the presence of God.

LETTERS TO QUEEN MELISANDE OF JERUSALEM

Melisande, daughter of King Baldwin II of Jerusalem, was the rightful heir to the throne upon her father's death, although before her marriage to Fulk V of Anjou, her betrothed negotiated with Baldwin for the right to serve as co-regent with her. Upon Fulk's death in 1143 in a hunting accident, Melisande became the sole ruler, albeit under the title of Regent Queen. The loss of the city of Edessa to the Muslims instigated the Second Crusade. Although her crown was seen as a regency in the eyes of European aristocracy, evidence suggests the Muslim leaders regarded her as a rightful monarch, even negotiating with her for prisoner exchanges.[6]

Four letters from Bernard to Queen Melisande exist (*Ep 206, 289, 354, 355*). *Letter 206* is a letter of commendation for one of Bernard's relatives who was arriving in Jerusalem to help secure the kingdom. Bernard asks the queen to care for him as she has for the other relatives of the abbot who had presented themselves before her. Not simply writing to recommend his

---

6. Usamah, *An Arab-Syrian Gentleman and Warrior*, 110.

relative to Melisande, Bernard has spiritual counsel, as well. He encourages her to ensure that the pleasures of the flesh and the power of the throne do not hinder her spiritual progress. Bernard asks, "What do you benefit if you reign for a few days on earth and to have been deprived of the kingdom of heaven (Matt 16:26)?" To actualize her activity in this heavenly kingdom, he exhorts her to care for the pilgrims, the needy, even the Muslim prisoners, for "in such sacrifices is God's favor obtained." Exhorting care for the Islamic captives is consistent with Bernard's exhortations during the recruitment of the Second Crusade not to persecute the Jews. For Bernard, those who appear sinful or who are marginalized in society are still persons deserving of the reception of God's love. Bernard encourages Melisande to heed his counsel, for unlike others who offer her guidance, he writes as one who has an unselfish love for her.[7]

In *Letter 289* (1153) Bernard counsels Melisande that despite the increasing pressures of her reign, she should remain faithful by following the example of Christ, making "the Savior a wall for the protection of your conscience." He reminds her to not forget herself in the midst of her administration of her duties as queen, stating, "You will not rule well if you are not well ruled." Like each person created by God, Melisande must rule herself and be ruled by God. She rules herself through humility and self-knowledge. She is ruled by God when she submits herself to God because she has attained a healthy understanding of herself. Offering this type of spiritual counsel to a member of the laity is remarkable considering the cultural context in which Bernard was writing. Not only did Melisande have the spiritual capacity to follow this ideal, she had the ability to be ruled by Christ in the midst of her responsibilities as Queen of Jerusalem. Bernard expects her to live a life in Christ at a level of obedience similar to that of his monks. The only difference was her life situation and calling.

LETTER 244 TO EMPEROR CONRAD OF ROME (1146)

The first line of this important letter reveals Bernard's understanding of the relationship between church and state: "The Crown and the Priesthood could not be more sweetly, or amiably, or more completely united or planted together than in the person of the Lord." He further argues that the Crown and the Priesthood are as united in marriage as husband and wife, quoting Jesus in Matthew 19:6, "What God has joined together, let no

7. Sommerfeldt, *Bernard of Clairvaux: On the Life of the Mind*, 66.

one separate." Rather than simply united contractually, Bernard maintains the church and the Crown should be united spiritually, always seeking the best interest of the other. Married couples are united by God, yet they each have distinct roles. The same relationship exists between the church and the state. The implication of this relationship to Bernard's theology is quite clear. Because the pope represents Christ, the head of the church, the state must submit to the church as a wife is called to submit to her husband (*Ep* 5:22). The intimate relationship between the church and state exists spiritually, and like a marriage, never to be divorced from each other. By understanding this, Conrad will be able to serve Christ more faithfully in his own life and rule.

With this understanding of the marriage between church and state, Bernard interrogates Conrad regarding the violent actions of the Romans against Pope Eugenius: "If you have knowledge of this, how long will you impartially ignore their abuse and assault?" Because the church is under assault by the rebellious, prideful Roman people, Conrad has an obligation to support it. He exhorts Conrad to gird his sword upon his thigh and ensure justice is done.[8] Conrad has a spiritual responsibility to protect the church above his responsibilities to serve as the Emperor of Rome.

In conclusion, Bernard offers a word of warning and counsel to Conrad. He states if anyone should give him guidance that contrasts with what Bernard has shared, he does not love the king, does not appreciate the king's majesty, or else is seeking his own interests and not those of either God or the king (Phil 2:21). The authority with which Bernard writes to the Emperor rivals the language a pope might use. Because this letter is written during Eugenius' papacy, Bernard may have felt the necessity to write on behalf of his former monk. Once again, either Bernard may be exceeding his duties as the abbot of Clairvaux or else using his self-understood divine, rhetorical license to share what he believes is the will of God. Either way, Bernard took a risk of appearing to abuse his role in the church, potentially causing more harm than good in the situation.

LETTERS TO YOUNG MEN

Bernard had little patience for young men with great potential who, in his own determination, were not using their skills for God, but for their own

---

8. This theme is the same counsel Bernard gave to Pope Innocent II in *Ep* 161, which regards the murder of Archibald, sub-deacon of Orleans. *SBOp* 7:370.

ambitions. In his youth, Bernard would have found himself in the same situation as many of them. He did not accept the excuses they made regarding the postponement of their conversion, the settlement of financial affairs, concern about their parents welfare, or other matters. Initiating the process of conversion was vitally important for Bernard, as he believed that monastic conversion was the beginning of one's unity with God and a means of purification of the soul.[9] As a young nobleman, Bernard faced these same situations himself yet did not hesitate leaving all and entering Cîteaux. Knights and members of the lower nobility occupied the young Cistercian houses, and new recruits (based on the records that have survived) were almost exclusively young noblemen. Bernard's 'recruitment letters' to young men all suggest that these recruits came from distinguished families. These letters were later collected and then distributed as examples of issues that Cistercian novices might face.[10]

In several instances in these letters, Bernard refers to the lives of these young men as flowers, or possessing the quality of flowers.[11] On some occasions he refers to the "flower of their youth"[12] or the "glory of their youth."[13] In another letter, Bernard refers to their lives causing the cross of Christ "to bloom into flower."[14] These images are poignant, for as the lives of these young men are budding, they will soon blossom but then fade away. As the flowers mentioned in Isaiah 40:7 that bloom one day and the next day wither and fall, the lives of these young men are shorter than they realize.

LETTER 104 TO MASTER WALTER

From the context of this letter, Walter must have been a young man from a distinguished family. In this letter, Bernard warns the young man to flee from the notoriety of a strong education and professional secular career. The abbot writes, "Your mother wishes what will hinder your salvation, and through this impedes her own." Bernard recognizes the academic accomplishments of young Walter and admits that when combined with his noble birth, he had the potential to have much success in the secular world;

9. Farkasfalvy, "The First Step in the Spiritual Life: Conversion," 74–77.
10. Bouchard, *Sword, Miter, and Cloister*, 120.
11. *Ep* 411; *SBOp* 8:392.
12. *Ep* 112; *SBOp* 7:286.
13. *Ep* 104; *SBOp* 7:261.
14. *Ep* 109; *SBOp* 7:280.

however, he calls this a hollow pursuit, and a pursuit after what is passing, not eternal. Bernard refers to Walter's noble birth, graceful body, handsome appearance, and swift character, which are all notable qualities to have, but he warns Walter that to use them for oneself and not for the One who gave them is a sure way to face God's judgment. One might argue these characteristics may be similar to a description of young Bernard in the *Vita Prima*.[15] Bernard had nobility, education, and a promising career ahead of him but instead chose Cîteaux. He had little patience for similar young men who did not have the immediate inclination to do the same. Bernard's assumption was that when individuals come to a full understanding of who they are, they realize their need to follow Christ. His approach to directing souls was to help individuals see themselves with God's eyes.

Bernard asks Walter, "In whom, I ask you, does your worth lie, you who are made in the image of your Maker?" Finding one's worth in what one accomplishes makes Walter no better than a brute beast of the field known for its strength. Quoting John 6:27, Bernard exhorts that Walter should not labor for the food that perishes but for the food that has eternal life. Walter knows what he needs to do, and he should not allow any obstacles, including those from within his family, to stop him from fleeing from the world and pursue God. Walter needs to take an honest look at himself and his inner motivations. This decision is a major step in Walter fleeing the ambitions of the world and running to God. Only then will this young man be able to discern his true worth in the eyes of God, and not his worth as the world defines it.

Bernard writes from experience. He knows the pressure young Walter must be experiencing, for he chose Cîteaux rather than a more prestigious abbey such as Cluny. He did not surrender to the pressure, and neither should Walter. Unlike other situations in which Bernard offers counsel in areas totally unrelated to his life, this guidance is fatherly advice from a wise abbot who has actually been in Walter's circumstances. The letter is an attempt at offering spiritual counsel to a young man that Bernard desires to see bloom into spiritual maturity. Although Walter fears leaving his mother, Bernard will become his father and his mother if the young man would simply leave behind his riches and worldly promise. Forsaking his earthly mother, father, sisters and brothers for spiritual equivalents will secure his eternal salvation. He can only be faithful to Christ if he obeys Christ, for he cannot serve both the world and God.

15. *Vita Prima Bernardi.*

Letter 107 to Thomas, Provost of Beverly (before 1131)

Letter 107 is actually the second of two surviving letters written by Bernard to Thomas in an attempt to motivate him to fulfill his monastic promise. The first letter, *Letter 411* (1130), was written to encourage Thomas to fulfill a recent religious promise. In it, Bernard praises Thomas both for his strong character and love of poverty. When Bernard first wrote to Thomas, the abbot's tone was generally positive in nature, written with emotional vigor and a motivating style to encourage the young man to fulfill a monastic intent. It seems Thomas delayed his admission to Clairvaux, much to the disappointment of its abbot.

In *Letter 107*, Bernard's tone is noticeably different, and the text itself is much longer, as Bernard is obviously frustrated that Thomas has not yet entered the abbey. Bernard writes, "We long for your presence; indeed we have demanded your promised and desired presence." Bernard argues that Thomas and others like him do not want to leave the world, for they have made the world their friend. Befriending the world makes befriending the Bridegroom impossible.[16] Thomas' personal desires were keeping him from being friends with God.

Seemingly leaving Thomas' specific situation behind, Bernard extemporaneously begins a scripture-laden diatribe against those who rely on the world for their spiritual sustenance. "Woe to you, sons of this world, foolish in prudence, ignorant of the saving Spirit, not sharing in the counsels that gush forth from the Father and the Son." Because those who love the world cannot hear the Son crying out to them, the Son disguises his voice as he did the meaning of the parables to the masses. Thomas' failure to fulfill his monastic promise is characteristic of the selfish ambition of others, even clergy. Renewal of the church begins with the renewal of individuals within the church. Bernard does not wish to see the Bride of Christ littered with unfaithful members. Whether he wants to admit it or not, Thomas' personal ambitions affect the whole of the church.

Although he is undoubtedly frustrated with Thomas, the abbot still refers to him as his *carissime*. He implores Thomas to open his ears to Christ.[17] Bernard uses the illustration that just as the parents of the child Jesus were unable to find him among their friends and relations, Thomas must follow their example by departing his own friends and family in order

16. See *SC* 70.8–9. *SBOp* 1:212.
17. Kereszky, "Relationship between Anthropology and Christology," 286.

to find Christ.[18] He ends the long letter with a word of hope: For the time being Bernard will still allow Thomas to refer to him as his abbot but only as a matter of formality. Once Thomas enters Clairvaux, Bernard will be to him more than an abbot. He will be Thomas' fellow disciple whom the young man has chosen to be his abbot. Bernard knows the letter has been difficult, so he is determined to end the letter with the grace and love of God that is available to the young man. Bernard was undoubtedly frustrated with Thomas, but his unflinching concern was the state of Thomas' soul. Unfortunately, Thomas was unable to fulfill his monastic vow by entering Clairvaux because he died suddenly. The evidence is speculative as to whether or not he even received this letter.

LETTER 109 TO GEOFFREY OF PÉRONNE (1131)

If Thomas of Beverly serves as an example not to follow in making a monastic vow, then Geoffrey of Péronne serves as a positive contrast. Geoffrey was one of more than two dozen young men whom Bernard converted while on an excursion through Flanders. Later, Geoffrey became the Prior of Clairvaux and was nominated by both Bernard and Eugenius III to the See of Tournai. *Letter 109* is a congratulatory letter written to encourage Geoffrey and his companions to enter Clairvaux immediately before they could be tempted to delay their admission. Bernard was one of nearly thirty people who entered Cîteaux together, making him quite able to empathize with these young men. In a hyperbolic statement, Bernard begins the letter by stating that news of their conversion has caused the entire church to rejoice. Bernard contrasts them to those whom he calls *filiis diffidentiae* who put off their conversion from day to day, some of whom died unexpectedly and dropped into the pit of hell.[19] In contrast to those who made a monastic promise but failed to act upon it, Bernard describes Geoffrey and his companions as persons of holiness and valor:

> The glory of the world has been deemed as worthless, the flower
> of their youth has been trampled, their nobility has not been taken
> into account, the wisdom of the world has been declared as folly,
> flesh and blood has not been assented to, the affections of loving

18. Bernard makes this same argument in *Ep* 412 (*SBOp* 8:394-95), addressed "To my beloved son T-," which contains many of the same themes found in *Ep* 107 to Thomas of Beverly (*SBOp* 7:267-276).

19. A possible reference to Thomas, Provost of Beverly.

parents has been rejected, the favors, and the honors and digni-
ties of the world have been considered as excrement so they might
gain Christ.

Bernard writes all that remains for these dear sons of his is to have the
perseverance necessary to put their intention into effect and enter Clairvaux. Their abbot-to-be pledges to help them in their spiritual progress by
placing their burdens on his shoulders, which have already been bent in
prayer for them.[20] Bernard endeavors for them to understand his role in
their lives as a spiritual shepherd. They may be leaving the comforts of the
world, but they are entering a holy land where they will be received with a
hero's welcome.

From the tone of this and other letters to young men, the influence
Bernard had in recruiting them for Clairvaux is perspicaciously clear.
One can imagine a young nobleman hearing Bernard preach an eloquent
and emotionally laded sermon on the sanctity and spiritual ecstasies of
Cistercian life, and then finding himself emotionally drawn to making a
vocational intent. Following Bernard's departure, and after the emotionalism has subsided, the young nobleman realizes that life within the walls of
monastery does not seem as enlightening as Bernard made it appear. While
his desire is to refocus his life on his preparations as a nobleman of France,
he finds Bernard will not release him from his commitment and threatens
him with the pit of hell if he does not acquiesce. Bernard definitely had a
gift for motivational conversion sermons, but the sermons' effects could
have produced emotionalism in the hearts of the hearers rather than the
voice of God.

LETTERS TO MARRIED COUPLES

Although letters to married couples are rare in Bernard's epistolary corpus,
their importance lies in what they present regarding his understanding of
Christian marriage. What may be the most engrossing aspect of these letters to married couples is that they exist at all. Bernard could have very
easily written to the husband singularly; however, by simply addressing
letters to both husband and wife, Bernard is affirming the role and sanctity

20. This symbolism is reminiscent of Part 2, Chapter 7 of Pope Gregory's *Pastoral
Rule*, in which the pope describes the spiritual burden and sacrifices involved in the
spiritual care of others.

of Christian marriage.[21] In fact, the abbot affirms that the freedom of love between husband and wife reflects the freedom that lovers of Christ have in a faith relationship.[22] Bernard is not silent in speaking of the holy union of man and woman, nor does he disparage the role of women in the life of men. Instead, he clearly maintains that God himself calls some people to marriage. In addition, in a minor way his letters to married couples also affirm the equality of God's love for both men and women and the place of women in the church.

Letter 110 to the Parents of Geoffrey of Péronne (1131)

When Geoffrey of Péronne and his companions made a profession to enter Clairvaux, Bernard applauded them for not placing their parents between themselves and Christ. *Letter 110* demonstrates the compassion Bernard felt for the parents of young men of promise who forsook their family estates and political responsibilities for the cloister. In this letter, Bernard writes to Geoffrey's parents to console and encourage them on the loss of their son.

The style of *Letter 109* to Geoffrey is dramatically different from this letter. While the former contains graphic images meant to inspire and promote action in the reader's life, the latter is meant to console. Both letters demonstrate Bernard's expansive grammatical skills. Bernard writes to Geoffrey's parents, "If you love him, you will certainly rejoice, for he walks to the Father, and how great a Father!" Rather than criticizing the paternal skills of Geoffrey's earthly father, Bernard praises the wondrous nature of the young man's eternal Father; for Geoffrey's best interest is to be with his eternal Father rather than his temporal parents. Rather than losing a son, Bernard writes the couple is actually gaining many sons, just as Geoffrey will be gaining many brothers at Clairvaux. In fact, the abbot writes, "All of us at Clairvaux or of Clairvaux receive him as a brother and you as our parents."[23]

Bernard concludes the letter by ensuring Geoffrey's parents that he himself will care for the young monk and will be to him a father, a mother, a sister, and a brother. They should be encouraged about their son's situation,

21. Sommerfeldt, "Bernard of Clairvaux on Love and Marriage," 142.

22. Leclercq, *Monks on Marriage*, 28.

23. By 1131, when this letter was written, Bernard had begun to refer to the Cistercians as being of Clairvaux rather than of Cîteaux.

for although Cistercian life is harsh, "he is going quickly to joy and not mourning." Rather than losing an earthly family, Geoffrey has gained a heavenly one, for Clairvaux was a foretaste of heaven. Geoffrey's admission into Clairvaux serves as an example of the faithfulness of an individual to relinquish the world and his own desires in order to follow Christ. His parents should rejoice that their son has chosen this road. Their own faithfulness in releasing their son will even have eternal consequences for them, for in this act they demonstrate humility and obedience to Christ.

Letter 421 to Mar and his wife

At times, the salutations of Bernard's letters are as interesting as the contents of the letters. Such is the case of *Letter 421* to Mar and his wife, which begins, "Bernard, Abbot of Clairvaux, to his beloved friend Mar and his wife, that they will love each other, but not to prefer their mutual love to their love of Christ." The salutation in itself encapsulates Bernard's theology of marriage and offers the couple spiritual counsel. While they are God's gifts to each other, they must never allow this human love to interfere with their love for God, for their true spouse was Christ. No human connection should supersede one's commitment to Christ, for union with the holy remains the most intimate relationship attainable by humanity.

Letter 421 is a brief letter, written to encourage a man and his wife to continue giving alms. He begins the argument by stating the uncertain nature of society dictates that eventually they will lose their possessions. Bernard encourages them to send their possessions to heaven by giving them to the poor. He entreats them to give their possessions to those who need them more than they do. He even states God may have multiplied the miseries of the poor simply to afford Mar and his wife the endless joy of giving and to secure their salvation. In fact, their faithfulness to each other and to the poor around them will affect the entire church—not only by example, but also through their faithfulness to the life God has called them to live.

Bernard encourages Mar and his wife to recommend the same counsel to their acquaintances and even names specific individuals for them to approach. After inviting them to Clairvaux, he ends the letter. Although this letter seems simple, a closer inspection reveals a fascinating theological and spiritual approach by Bernard. Despite the separation between the roles of the lay and the clergy in Bernard's society, in this instance the abbot is recruiting this lay couple for the work of ministry. As Bernard instructed them to give alms to the poor, they are now empowered to do the same for other laypersons. Bernard utilized this method in another letter, when he approved as valid the baptism of a dying infant performed by a peasant.[24]

Through this seemingly minor letter, Bernard is affirming the ministerial role of the laity in an age when the clergy held most, if not all, of the spiritual authority and responsibility. Although the spiritual responsibility he offers them is limited, Bernard recognizes, affirms, and charges this married couple with the task of sharing with others directives for a faithful spiritual life. Through this simple exhortation, Bernard clarifies two assumptions about his view of the laity. First, he believes laity have the capacity to encourage one another spiritually. Second, he affirms the holiness of Christian marriage and affirms the place of marriage in the church.

LETTERS TO OTHER LAITY

At times Bernard addressed letters to the people of an entire town or diocese. During the papal schism, for example, he wrote letters of instruction and spiritual warning to the people of Genoa (*Letter 129*) and the people of Pisa (*Letter 130*). To support the expedition against the heretics in Eastern Europe, he addressed *Letter 457* "To all the faithful." When the Roman people rebelled against the Cistercian pope Eugenius III, Bernard wrote *Letter 243* to scold them back into submission. Sometimes, as in the advent of Bernard's arrival in a village or town, he would write a letter to prepare them for his visit. *Letter 242* is one such letter.

LETTER 242 TO THE PEOPLE OF TOULOUSE (1145)

Bernard begins the letter by congratulating them on their opposition to heretics. He references his previous visit with them to confront a heretic named Henry, and the positive outcomes they experienced together, including the witness of God's miraculous power. He encourages them to remain vigilant against anyone who would question the authority of the church or denigrate the reality of the presence of Christ's body and blood in

---

24. *Ep* 403; *SBOp* 8:383–84. The peasant baptized the infant with these words: "I baptize you in the name of God and of the holy and true cross." Bernard's argument for the validity of the baptism is that although the peasant did not know the proper ritual, God knew the man's heart.

the Eucharist. He encourages the people of Toulouse to "pursue them and arrest them . . . because it is not safe to sleep near serpents." He encourages the people to be faithful to their bishop and other superiors of the church and to be active in hospitality. Following the examples of Abraham and Lot, they should receive not angels but the Lord of the angels who comes to them in the appearance of strangers, taking care of their physical needs. Although they live secular lives, they still have a responsibility to live in an awareness of spiritual realities. They represent Christ to others. As God has given himself to them, they are to give themselves to others.

In a final exhortation, Bernard reminds them not to receive any preacher among them unless that person has documentation that he has been sent directly from the pope himself or who has permission from the bishop to preach.[25] Describing these heretics, Bernard writes, "They clothe themselves in piety but thoroughly deny its power, and mix profane novelties of speech and understanding with heavenly words, like venom and honey." They should avoid them like poison, for they are ravenous wolves.

Similar to Bernard's presuppositions regarding the role of the laity in *Letter 421*, Bernard affirms the aptitude of the laity to recognize and eradicate heretics from their midst. The people of Toulouse have already achieved this in the past, and he encourages them to persevere in the same manner into the future. Although Bernard exhorts them to welcome only those traveling preachers who have documentation from Rome, he acknowledges that they have the discernment to recognize a heretic by the nature of the message he preaches. Knowing right Eucharistic theology is a responsibility the people should possess. In fact, their theological discernment and comprehension actually serves to support the role of the church superiors. Once again, Bernard stresses the capacity for the laity to possess spiritual and theological discernment. All followers of Christ, despite their vocational station, are called to obedience and spiritual responsibility.

LETTER 292 TO A CERTAIN LAYMAN

Letter 292 regards a monk of Clairvaux named Peter, whose relative has been encouraging him to leave Clairvaux and return to the world. Bernard is writing this letter on behalf of the poor monk and offers a controlled

---

25. Bernard was probably referring to renegade monks Arnold of Brescia and Henry of Lausanne.

rebuke to his relative that culminates in the abbot extending an invitation for the relative to make a monastic vocation himself.

Bernard chides the man for attempting to dissuade a soldier of Christ from the service of his Lord. He is astonished that this relative of the monk Peter would add temptations to how the devil is already tempting Peter on a daily basis. Bernard states that although he could add more condemnations to the man's actions, he will not return evil for evil. Instead, he will pray for the man, desire a better attitude in the man's life, and impart both in the current letter. Although this man is causing turmoil in the life of a young monk, Bernard offers him spiritual guidance by the very nature of this letter. The monk's abbot certainly had the rhetorical acumen to burst forth with a plethora of hyperbolic rebukes. However, Bernard has the discernment to use a different rhetorical approach to reach this relative.

Bernard deduces that the primary reason for the layperson's temptations of Peter is that he is not wise in the ways of God. He would have this godly wisdom if only he was "dreading the horror of the depths, seeking the things above, and scorning what is at your hand." Bernard offers the same counsel to Pope Eugenius III in *On Consideration*.[26] Offering the same spiritual counsel to a pope and to a layperson demonstrates Bernard's theological conclusion that human nature is constant, regardless of vocation or faithfulness. Certainly Bernard held that Eugenius was more faithful to Christ than this relative who was encouraging a soldier of Christ to run in retreat from a spiritual battle. The human condition is unvarying, despite obedience or disobedience to Christ. Each person must understand who they are, who is above them, what is below them, and the situation around them. Contrary to Eugenius, who needed a simple reminder of this life-awareness, the recipient of *Letter 292* must be introduced to the importance of a multi-dimensional understanding of his life. Bernard is able to have compassion on this man, for this relative of the monk Peter simply does not understand himself. His view of Christ is being blocked by his hidden ambitions.

The abbot desires to remain on friendly terms with the man, for he would enjoy leading the man to salvation. Bernard believes that hope exists for this meddlesome relative to attain a Christ-awareness in his life, so he words the letter carefully, unlike other letters in which he assails the recipient with a verbal diatribe. Bernard had the capacity for extended grace; even to someone whom he believed was being used by the devil. By ceasing his

26. *Csi* 2.6; *SBOp* 3:414.

current activity of deceit and temptation, this man can actually contribute to the ministry not only of his relative Peter, but also to the greater church, as well. Bernard desires this man to know that his actions affect far more people than just his monastic relative. The abbot calls him into account for potentially infecting the entire church with his devilish actions.

CONCLUSIONS

In writing to laypersons, Bernard was essentially writing to individuals in the world he left when he entered Cîteaux. Because his flight from the world in reality was an engagement with the world through his many forays and interventions, he found himself able to navigate through the world of secular politics quite effectively. Bernard's confidence in his political acumen regarding the affairs of state was ambitious, if not naive. In his estimation, the truest form of Christian discipleship was at Clairvaux, the "true Jerusalem," and anyone who made a monastic profession should, like the disciples of Jesus, leave their nets at once and follow. Regardless of the tremendous amount of political and familial responsibilities these future novices had to relinquish before being admitted, the abbot had little patience when someone delayed a promise to Christ.

Clearly, Bernard did not believe one had to live a monastic life to be a faithful follower of Christ. He believed Christ calls all individuals from all stratum of society to live faithfully where God has placed them. Living faithfully to Christ in secular society was theoretically possible, although without the same assurance. Those in secular society certainly had the capacity for a life of complete faithfulness to God.[27] However, Bernard also believed that the surest way to attain salvation was through a monastic vocation.

In a certain sense, Bernard's letters to laity serve as his attempt at spiritual direction in the secular world. Although he understood that he was not the abbot of the laity to whom he wrote letters, he felt a responsibility to share his message of humility, obedience, and self-understanding with them. While he can be accused of naïvely assuming that all persons shared his assumptions regarding the importance of monasticism to the church, his letters to laity serve as spiritual instruction manuals for people whose daily activities did not always center on a life in Christ.

27. Sommerfeldt, *Bernard of Clairvaux: On the Life of the Mind*, 58.

Through these important letters in Bernard's correspondence, scholars can understand more completely Bernard's ecclesiology and his activity outside of Clairvaux. The Kingdom of God extended far beyond the church's jurisdiction. All who reside under the church's care have a place in God's Kingdom and the capacity to grow spiritually, although the monastery is the surest means to salvation. Laity, whether married or celibate, have a role in the restoration of the church through the reformation of their own souls to the image of Christ. Through self-awareness and understanding, they can strive to live in humble obedience. Bernard correspondence to laity is much more than mere supplication for benevolent gifts. The abbot had a spiritual agenda, as well. Whether writing to kings or to young maidens, Bernard felt obligated to the welfare of all, and to the health of the Kingdom of God.

CHAPTER 9

Bernard's Letters as a Methodology for Twelfth-Century Ecclesiastical Reform

THE LETTERS OF BERNARD of Clairvaux, although written primarily to address specific crises and situations that held importance to him, contain an abundance of spiritual insights that have transcended time and culture. These documents are not merely items of historical record but serve as examples of Bernard's deeper reformation and restoration ideals, both corporate and personal. Through his letters, Bernard engaged in directing souls in order to fulfill his desire of restoring the church to its apostolic priorities through the individual faithfulness of each person in the church.

The process of letter writing was a fundamental aspect of Bernard's vocation. His letters were written to individuals from all strata of society with hope that the recipients would heed the abbot's counsel; counsel that Bernard believed was coming from God. Although the subject matter of the letters covers dozens of diverse topics, this study has shown common themes woven throughout the corpus that summarize the abbot's epistolary objectives. While the nature of these themes is in no way limited to Bernard's letters, it is through his letters that he offers a practical application of the theoretical topics in his treatises, sermons, and discourses.

THEMES OF SPIRITUAL DIRECTION IN BERNARD'S LETTERS

Summarizing a corpus of letters with such diversity as Bernard's hardly seems plausible. His letters span several decades and are addressed to more than a hundred individuals and covering dozens of topics. Despite this daunting task, a close examination of his letters reveals that significant spiritual themes emerge. This study has demonstrated that through the medium of letter writing, Bernard desired to achieve goals that lie beneath the circumstances for writing the letters. Letters were his platform to achieve his agendas in the church. Yet, on a much deeper level, his letters also reveal his concern for the spiritual well-being of everyone who received his letters. These concerns can be summarized in five basic themes.

The Vice of Personal Ambition

As a child of the Middle Ages, Bernard certainly believed in the stability of the roles in the strata of society. For him, personal ambition demonstrates nothing more than pride, which is the opposite of Christian charity. Ambition can manifest itself in a monk seeking a less disciplined life, as in *Letter 1* to Robert. Bernard also saw ambition in abbots who tired of their responsibilities, as in the letters to Arnold of Morimond or *Letter 141* to Humbert, Abbot of Igny. By not taking their abbatial responsibilities seriously as shepherds of poor sheep, they placed themselves before their monks. This egregious attitude was no better than if they had purposefully sought a bishopric for themselves. Bernard sees in the office of abbot neither a personal privilege nor a stepping-stone for an ecclesiastic career but a duty to care for the ones entrusted to his care, especially the weak, the novices and monks of new establishments, even when doing so harms one's own spiritual life.[1]

Directing the soul of another demands sacrifice, which is the opposite of ambition. Understood this way, any aspect of personal vocational ambition was sinful to Bernard. First, it made one's supposed needs the center of life instead of the needs of others. For example, offering spiritual counsel to a monk in order to achieve vocational fulfillment is merely using the monk for one's own actualization. Second, personal ambition doubted the hand and will of God in the process of one being placed in his or her current vocational position. Seeking a higher ecclesiastical position doubts God's wisdom in calling a person to his or her vocational placement. The implication of this attitude is the person becoming more important than the church. The church is not comprised of individuals, but persons. Each person's actions synthesize with the actions of other persons in the church.

---

1. Pfeifer, "Klosterstreitigkeiten?," 468.

Personal ambition, according to Bernard, hinders this organic flow of the Holy Spirit in the church.

In his letters to bishops, Bernard emphasized that they seek the welfare of their flock rather than their own interests. This was for the sake of those in the diocese as well as for their own sake. A primary example of this is *Letter 26* to Guy, Bishop of Lausanne, in which Bernard stresses the need for the cardinal virtues in Guy's life as a means of remembering himself and the people to whom he was called to serve. In *Letter 329* Bernard warns the Bishop of Limoges of the wiles of the Bishop of Rodez, whose only concern was his own ambition, to the detriment of not only the people in his diocese, but of the entire church.

Bernard had the confidence to counsel popes and to make judgments regarding their agendas. The letters of Bernard to Innocent II and Eugenius III are ripe with examples of the abbot of Clairvaux appearing to scold the pontiffs for either taking or not taking action, both of which Bernard believed to stem from personal ambition. In *Letter 178*, for example, Bernard warns Innocent II that he must put aside his own plans, for righteousness is perishing in the church. The pope's responsibility is not to focus on political affairs, but the holiness of the church. *Letter 268* concerns Bernard's shock at Eugenius' elevation of an individual that Bernard believes to be of questionable character. The abbot questions the pope's motivations for the decision, stating that this sinful action resulted from poor counsel and ambition.[2]

The laity were not exempt from Bernard's criticism, either. Most prominent of these letters are those written to young men who had promised themselves to Clairvaux yet never entered. By placing their own desires before their promise to God, they were in danger of eternal damnation, for if Christ were their life, they would have, following the example of Peter and Andrew, immediately left their nets to follow Jesus. For those in political leadership, their attitude of servanthood was an example to those in a subservient position. Bernard had a close relationship with King Louis VII of France, particularly since the young king strived to live a devout life; however, Bernard took advantage of his relationship with the king through a biting letter (*Letter 220*) when he believed the king to be acting selfishly against Count Theobald of Champagne, Bernard's primary benefactor. Had

2. In Bernard's treatise to Eugenius, *On Consideration*, the abbot reminds the pope that the church of their day is full of ambitious people. The church, he writes, shudders at these ambitious men as a cave shudders at the spoils that hiding thieves have taken from travelers. *Csi* 1.13; *SBOp* 3:409.

the king placed the ambitions of God before his own, Louis would have been in a much more stable political situation, for his actions resulted in social unrest. He was now suffering the implications of his own vice.

For Bernard, personal ambition is a tangible demonstration of an individual not possessing a complete self-understanding, for self-knowledge leads one to seek God's desires for one's life. "I am not agitated by undeserved blame," he wrote to Cardinal Haimeric, "nor do I accept undue praise."[3] The importance of possessing an honest self-perception was important to Bernard, for it allowed an individual to hear more clearly the voice of God.

He did not object to people rising through the ecclesiastical ranks, or moving between strata of society, as long as it was God's will. Although Bernard himself rejected an archbishopric (and thus could himself be accused of self-ambition by desiring to remain abbot of Clairvaux), he did so in the unshakable confidence he had in God's purposes for his life. Thus, in Bernard's mind his rejection of the archbishopric was a demonstration of his faithfulness to God, despite the fact that others could have been heeding the will of God by offering him the prestigious position. His apparent ambivalent tendencies made Bernard a polarizing figure in his day, although his personal charm and charismatic personality often made up for his inconsistencies.[4]

The Role of Obedience as a Means of Faithfulness to Christ

If self-understanding in Bernard is a means to humility, then humility is the means to faithfulness to God. Faithfulness to Christ is demonstrated through obedience to both earthly and heavenly authorities. This spiritual counsel is a theme is found in nearly every one of Bernard's letters, as he persuaded everyone, from popes to laity, to live faithfully to the position in which God has placed them. He exhorted Pope Eugenius to live faithfully to his Cistercian vocation, despite the many pressures placed upon him by the nature of his office. Kings and Queens needed to pay homage and stand humbly before the King of Kings, whom they merely served. Monks, abbots, and bishops should be obedient to Christ, their example, and to their earthly superiors. All laity must serve their nobles as they would serve Christ.

3. *Ep* 48; *SBOp* 7:138.
4. Leclercq, *Bernard of Clairvaux and the Cistercian Spirit*, 9.

Despite the importance of living obediently in the corporate community of Christ, Bernard believed the necessity of being obedient to oneself was far more important. This involved a healthy self-understanding that was the basis for loving God. Obedience to Christ is achieved through love of Christ, not force, and as creatures formed in the *imago Dei,* we have the ability and the freedom to choose an obedient life. Bernard believed that his actions in the world were a demonstration of his own obedience to Christ, for despite his longing for solace and seclusion (particularly near the end of his life), he found himself being continually summoned by others to intervene on their behalf.

Obedience to oneself required self-discipline, a trait that Bernard expected everyone to be able to possess. He was quite impatient with individuals who did not immediately enter Clairvaux after devoting themselves to the abbot, which perhaps originated from Bernard's self-perceived role as an external motivator in their lives. Both the discipline afforded by the monastic community's strict code of obedience and an individual's openness to the working of the Holy Spirit in his or her life facilitated self-discipline, which began with a healthy understanding of one's self. For Bernard, obedience and faithfulness to Christ leads to love, which for Bernard is the primary motivating desire a human can express. Love for oneself, love for God, and love for others is the effect of faithful obedience. The biblical mandate for Christians to lay down their lives for God and for others grows from a seed of humble obedience to God. This exhortation for love encompasses not only monasticism, but also the realm of secular rulers.[5]

THE HARMONY OF CHURCH AND STATE

A third major theme in Bernard's letters regards the harmony of church and state. The Bride of Christ for Bernard is the whole of Christian society working together to achieve God's objectives in the world. Although different roles exist in the church, we are all the same Bride.[6] Both swords, spiritual and temporal, belong to the church, although the spiritual sword is used *by* the church and the temporal sword is used *for* the church. Together, the two swords constitute the faithful Bride of Christ.

---

5. In *Ep* 224, Bernard writes that the King of France broke a pact of friendship with Count Theobald of Champagne, and act which violates the king's responsibility to spread the love of God to those in his kingdom. *SBOp* 8:91–3.

6. *SC* 76.8; *SBOp* 1:259.

The abundance of letters written to temporal authorities demonstrates his belief in the importance of the state to the church, and the affective relationship each has to the spiritual health of the other. For example, in *Letter 288*, written to his uncle Andrew, a Knight of the Temple, Bernard criticizes the princes of France for their godless behavior in the Second Crusade. Their selfishness and disobedience to Christ while on the Crusade had a direct effect on the disastrous outcome of the Crusade. Had their intentions been for the good rather than for evil, Christian victory could have been theirs. Perhaps his sometimes biting criticism of secular authorities (e.g., Stephen, King of England and Roger, King of Sicily) is that these royal servants of God had forgotten their duty to serve the King of Kings. Rather than taking part in the life of the Bride, they were striving against the Bride, causing her distress. Bernard's lack of hesitation in offering spiritual counsel to secular rulers demonstrates his belief that they had an important role in the church by serving the Christ through the interests of the church. Because these temporal leaders had a role in the church, each of them possessed the innate capacity to live faithfully for God by minimizing the effects of the world in their lives. Through his letters, Bernard desired to become their spiritual guide, despite the fact that as a monk, his life was quite dissimilar culturally to theirs.

No matter of state is independent from the church. Whether dealing with the care of widows, the settling of peasant debts, or the stealing of pigs, God has placed the rulers on the earth by God's power and for God's sake, that they might encourage good, restrain evil, defend the poor, and offer justice to the downtrodden.[7] In fact, the charity they offer to others should be seen as offering charity to Christ himself. The letters of petition Bernard writes to both lay and ecclesiastical authorities are surprisingly similar: he reminds them of their duty as servants of Christ and asks them to intervene on behalf of one who has been treated unjustly.[8] Both sacred and secular rulers have the same spiritual expectations, as well. In a manner similar to the way he exhorts Bishop Guy of Lausanne to allow the cardinal virtues to become part of his life, he encourages Queen Melisande of Jerusalem to live

---

7. For example, see *Ep* 39; *SBOp* 7:97–8; *Ep* 279; *SBOp* 8:191.

8. The only distinguishing aspect of these letters is the nature of the person whose plight Bernard is petitioning: to ecclesiastical leaders he usually writes on behalf of monks, abbots, or bishops; to secular leaders he usually writes on behalf of laity.

in the same manner, exhibiting fortitude, prudence, justice, and temperance in her rule as Queen.[9]

Bernard's ecclesiology is tightly bound with his Christology in that the incarnational nature of Christ on earth remains through the Holy Spirit in the church, which serves Christ incarnationally through charity and holiness. Every person, regardless of their station in life, has a role in the Body of Christ, for Christ died for all people that they might freely choose to become part of Christ's body. Since both the surest way to Christ and the health of the church were through the spiritual health of the monasteries, everyone in the Body of Christ should support monastic reform. If one was not called to a monastic vocation, then they should make benefices to monasteries near them. Since God uses all people in the body of Christ, all people in the church must work in harmony, with a spirit of charity, to be a faithful church on earth as the church is faithful in heaven.

A Return to the Church of the Apostles

In a Letter 238 to Eugenius, Bernard reveals his hopes for the church when he says, "Who will grant me before I die to see the church of God as she was in the days of old (Isa 519): when the apostles extended their nets to catch not silver or gold, but to capture the souls of people (Matt 4:19)?" In the same letter, he exhorts Eugenius not to tear down the tree planted by his Heavenly Father. The church is a tree planted by God and nurtured by those who have gone before. The pope's responsibility is to ensure that the tree stays healthy and continues to grow. This was Bernard's understanding of the function of the church: not to be consumed with material gain, but to be consumed with Christ's love for people.

Bernard's understanding of the church as the Bride of Christ impelled him to seek ecclesiastical perfection on earth, since the church represents Christ on earth. His ideal church was the church of the Fathers, and he draws upon them consistently throughout his works. Although he doubted Eugenius' ability to fulfill his papal duties, Bernard believed that the hand of God was at work to elevate his former monk as pope. While he feared for the pope's spiritual health and ability to fulfill the many responsibilities of Rome, he also knew of his own influence in the church and political skills, seeing an opportunity to steer the church in a direction that stressed the spiritual over the material.

9. Cf. Bernard's *Ep* 26 to Guy (*SBOp* 7:79) with *Ep* 254 to Melisande (*SBOp* 8:297-98).

Bernard's conservative views and ideology earned him the title "the last of the Fathers." Certainly the Fathers, particularly Gregory "the Great" and Augustine, influenced both his language and his understanding of the church. Bernard defends the honor of the church Fathers, particularly when their doctrine was affronted. He accuses Peter Abelard and Arnold of Brescia, for example, of "beating the Doctors of the church black and blue" by disparaging their writings in favor of modern philosophies. Bernard went so far as to place himself in the tradition of the church Fathers when he accused these two scholars of the very heretical views condemned by Fathers themselves.[10]

Scholasticism was beginning to flower in the twelfth century, as education moved from the monasteries to the academies, particularly in Paris. Bernard's distaste for any learning that does not lead to love resulted from his belief that Holy Scripture was the source for the knowledge of God. The abbot's use of scripture is so extensive that at times one finds it difficult to distinguish between his ideas and quotations from the Bible. As it was for many medieval ecclesiastic leaders, Bernard's knowledge of the Bible was so extensive that it became instinctive. For Bernard, the Bible leads to God, who is love. The knowledge of the universities leads to pride, or rather the temptation for pride, for it involves the use of curiosity, which is the first step on the ladder of pride. The church of old had no formal universities, but only the Scriptures, yet found the ability to construct theology both clearly and logically. The Apostolic church put its energies and finances in saving of souls, not in the maintenance of a complicated institution. This is the church to which Bernard desired to return.

Bernard may have had a nostalgic view of the apostolic Fathers, viewing their era as the 'glory days' of the church. In his mind, the Fathers were Christians of one heart, mind, and purpose, continuing the work of Christ as demonstrated by the apostles. In Bernard's view, the bloated church of the twelfth century had digressed to an entirely different understanding of itself than it had in the *diebus antiquis*. Although his tireless efforts found some minor success during his lifetime, he was a man who sought the impossible. However, Bernard had a spiritual ideal for the church; an ideal he attempted to see realized through the spiritual counsel of one person at a time.

---

10. He compares Abelard and Arnold to ancient heretics Arius, Nestorus, and Pelegius in *Epp* 330, 331, 332, 336 and 338.

An Integration of the Ecclesiastical and the Personal

Perhaps more than any other, *Letter 26* to Guy, Bishop of Lausanne serves as a model for Bernard's reformation ideal. From this letter, one sees that the union between ecclesiastical and personal discipline is a primary factor in Bernard's desires for the church. In fact, this synthesis is a theme throughout the entirety of the epistolary corpus. In his letters, Bernard admonishes abbots, monks, nobles, even popes for not taking seriously the nature of their position or not remembering their identities in Christ. Since the goal of the Christian life is love, both inner motivations and external fruit demonstrate an individual's faithfulness. While the former may be problematic to discern, it was, however, a major factor in Bernard's opinion of others. While some may have seen problems in this methodology, he saw nothing wrong in his approach of making judgments of people's motivations, even when he did not have full information about specific situations.

Although the summarization of the themes inherent in Bernard's epistolary corpus should not focus on a single, brief memo, *Letter 26* contains thematic elements of *regere animas* found in many of his letters. The abbot's instruction to Guy is to allow the cardinal virtues to dwell in his life so that he might be a faithful shepherd to the flock in his diocese. Letters found in each category of letter recipients contain components of this ideal. Inner faithfulness to Christ leads to external faithfulness to Christ. In other words, the capacity to become a good layperson, monk, abbot, bishop, pope, or king is contingent upon one's own relationship with Christ. The implication of this understanding is that personal sanctity is the means to achieve ecclesiastical sanctity.

In all levels of the church, this assumption of one affecting the whole is at work. A monk's obedience affects the obedience of other monks who live communally with him. An abbot's experience of Christ affects his ability to shepherd his monks. A monastery's collective obedience affects an entire order. The process continues through the various ecclesiastical strata. Bernard's desire was to offer spiritual counsel to individuals in all levels of the church in order to realize a faithful church for Christ. This task seems rather ambitious, but the abbot of Clairvaux believed he was merely the instrument of God's ambitions for the church in his day.

A THEMATIC SYNTHESIS

Emerging from these five, integrated themes is one primary idea that runs like a thread throughout Bernard's epistolary corpus. This foundational theme serves as a culmination of the five major themes: Regardless of the recipient of his letters, Bernard stresses the need for self-understanding as a means to Christlikeness. Without a healthy understanding of the self, one cannot fully grasp the concept of God's love. Furthermore, a healthy self-understanding leads one to humility, obedience, and an understanding of one's vocational call. Bernard attempted to stress this ideal through intentional *regere animas* in his epistolary activities.

In his letters to monks, Bernard understood that these men who had left the world to seek Christ could sometimes be conflicted as to their vocational call. His exhortation to them is to be obedient to Christ by submitting their wills to Christ's will. For example, in *Letter 1* to Robert, Bernard scolds his younger relative for leaving Clairvaux for Cluny because he allowed the Cluniacs to persuade him to leave a harsh life for an easier one. Had Robert possessed a more complete awareness of himself, this situation could have been averted. Bernard's letters to the monk Adam remind the wayward monk that his first obedience is to Christ, not a rebellious abbot. Had Adam understood himself as first a child of Christ and not a child of his abbot, he could have avoided a disastrous pilgrimage to Jerusalem. Monks vow obedience to their abbot, but they must understand that before they are monks, they are children of God.

In his letters to abbots, bishops, and popes (all men who possessed some sort of ecclesiastical authority), Bernard reminds them that in order to faithfully fulfill their responsibilities they must first learn how to master themselves. One example of this is *Letter 28* to Ardutio, Bishop-Elect of Geneva. Ardutio, a person Bernard believed to be lacking in the skills necessary to be a successful bishop, exhorts the bishop-elect that he should understand himself well enough to know that he needs competent assistants around him in order to fulfill the charges of a bishop. This self-awareness will keep him grounded and humble before Christ. Any ecclesiastical leader, whether a bishop, abbot or pope, must not forget his humble origins, for beneath his title and sometimes-silken garments is an individual who at one time was a simple priest or monk.

Self-knowledge as a child of God is a main theme in *Letter 136* to Innocent II, who had begun to question his identity in the papal schism of the 1130s. Bernard encourages Innocent to stay firm in his obedience and humility to God, and his papal identity will remain firm. Despite the political divide in the European church and governmental alliances formed around the two papal claimants, Bernard's exhortation to Innocent in this letter confirms that the abbot believed that since Innocent had a more thorough understanding of himself in relation to God and the church, he was the better candidate for pope.

In other letters to popes, Bernard reminds them that for the church to function as the faithful Body of Christ, it must have a healthy understanding of itself, as well. For example, *Letter 238* to Eugenius III contains Bernard's statement of longing for the church to exist as it did in the days of the apostles, when the focus of the church was not silver and gold, but the souls of people. The church had lost its way by losing its identity. Bernard's anthropology of the self has been transferred to his ecclesiology, for the church is both corporate and individual. Ecclesiastical leaders must assert the church's authority in the world without forgetting that the church and the state have a harmonious relationship.

Themes in his letters to laity synthesize into this idea of self-understanding, as well. Both peasants and kings, although they have different assigned roles in the world, are called by God to a life of faithfulness and obedience. Just as an ecclesiastic leader must understand both his and the church's role in the church, a secular leader must understand his role and the role of the state with regard to the church. A king may be the leader of a nation, but Christ the King serves as ruler of both the king's life and of the world.

Bernard wrote several letters to young men who had promised themselves to Clairvaux, but delayed their profession. On many occasions in these letters, Bernard stresses that if these men knew themselves and the tenuous nature of their souls, they would immediately flee their earthly comforts for the spiritual safety of the cloister. Bernard genuinely cared for the spiritual condition of these young men, and in the case of Thomas of Beverly (*Letter 108*), Bernard grieved for his soul, since the young man died before he made his profession.

Through this thematic synthesis, Bernard exhorts the recipients of his letters to remain faithful to themselves through humility, obedience, and charity. The actualization of these three in one's life materializes when that person can see him or herself through the eyes of God. Bernard used himself as a primary example of this methodology, for he firmly believed that because he understood his vocational calling and his identity as a humble child of God, the Spirit of God had enabled Bernard to be his mouthpiece to the world. The knowledge of the self is a primary consideration in Bernard's letters. Rather than understanding the self as an individual, Bernard desired that each person in the church understands him or herself as someone uniquely created in the *imago Dei*, yet created for community in the work of God in the world, the church.

CONCLUDING REMARKS

One can argue that a primary objective of Bernard's letters is the reform of the church. From his arrangement of the initial corpus to the content of the letters themselves, Bernard sought transformation in the church. Yet this reform, unlike the sixteenth-century reformers, was not to reform the system, but the people in the system. Although some have attempted to portray Bernard as a preliminary figure to the Protestant Reformation, Bernard was clearly Roman, supported the centrality of the church in Rome, and believed that the best reformation model for the church was monastic renewal. Yet, Bernard did not believe that everyone was called to a monastic vocation. They were called to live a holy life in whatever situation or class they found themselves. Of course, he believed the easiest way to live such a life was in the Cistercian monastery. Regarding the holiness of the general church, however, he maintained that extensive, radical reform could only take place if those who served in the various vocations in the church and in society lived holy, devout lives. According to Bernard, obedience, love, discipline, and faithfulness were virtues that that each person, regardless of their station in life, could attain through being faithful to Christ in whatever vocation God had called them to serve. Through his letters, Bernard attempted to usher in this holy paradigm across the Christian world.

Through the medium of letter-writing Bernard of Clairvaux attempted to bring the church back to Bridal purity through epistolary spiritual direction one person at a time. The faithfulness of the church was contingent upon the faithfulness of each Christian in the church. For ecclesiastical leaders, this responsibility was even more pronounced, for leaders were charged with the spiritual health of those they shepherded. Abbots, bishops, and popes carried the most spiritual responsibility, for they were placed in their respective positions by God. To seek another vocational position, with either greater or lesser responsibility, was to attempt to usurp the workings of the Holy Spirit. Bernard distinguishes between acceptable and unacceptable vocational movement. For the monk, the vow of stability could only be broken if the individual sought a more austere monastic lifestyle. Secular leaders had the task of stabilizing society in order for the church to be able to function properly. Like their ecclesiastical counterparts, secular leaders were called by God to their particular vocation. The only acceptable alteration of this calling was to seek a monastic vocation or a holy task, such as becoming a Templar or embarking upon a crusade.

Through the letters of Bernard of Clairvaux, scholars have the means to understand the man behind the image. Bernard the rhetorician did not hesitate to express his emotions in his letters; emotions that were at times joyful and encouraging, but also tempestuous, speculative, and even cynical. The Bernard of his letters is not a polished saint, but a saint stained with human nature. Perhaps this very character of his letters serves as a spiritual lesson unto itself: that the individual who strives to be holy must remember that he or she is first a human—formed in the *imago Dei*—seeking faithfulness to Christ with the whole of one's being. For Bernard, the restoration of the earthly church must first begin with the reformation of the individual soul.

Abbreviations for the Works
of Bernard of Clairvaux

SBOp   *Sancti Bernardi opera.* 8 vols. in 9. Edited by Jean Leclercq et al.
     Rome: Editiones Cistercienses, 1957–77.

Apo   *Apologia ad Guillelmum abbatem (Apology)*

Conv   *Sermo ad clericos de conversione (Sermons on Conversion)*

Csi   *De consideratione (On Consideration: Advice to a Pope)*

Dil   *De Diligendo Deo (On Loving God)*

Div   *Sermones de diversis (Occasional Sermons)*

Ep   *Epistola (Letters)*

Hum   *De gradibus humilitatis et superbiae (Steps of Humility and Pride)*

Lau   *Liber ad milites Templi De laude nouae militiae (In Praise of the
     New Knighthood)*

Prae   *Liber de praecepto et dispensatione (Book on Precept and
     Dispensation)*

Miss   *Sermones in laudibus Virginia Matris [Homiliae super "Missus est"
     in laudibus Virginis Matris] (Homilies in Praise of the Virgin Mary)*

Par   *Parabolae (The Parables)*

Qui   *Sermones super psalmum "Qui habitat" (Sermons on "He Who
     Dwells . . .")*

SC   *Sermo super Cantica canticorum (Sermons on the Song of Songs)*

Sent   *Sententiae (The Sentences)*

Asc   *Sermones in ascensione Domini (Sermons on Ascension)*

Gra   *Liber de gratia et de libero arbitrio (On Grace and Free Choice)*

Bibliography

Anderson, Luke. "Bernard of Clairvaux." In *Augustine through the Ages: An Encyclopedia*, edited by Allan D. Fitzgerald. Grand Rapids: Eerdmans, 1999.

Bamberger, John E. "The Monastic Vision of Saint Bernard of Clairvaux." *Monastic Studies* 19 (1991) 46–58.

Bouchard, Constance B. *Sword, Miter, and Cloister: Nobility and the Church in Burgundy, 980–1198*. Ithaca, NY: Cornell University Press, 1987.

Bredero, Adrian. *Bernard of Clairvaux: Between Cult and History*. Edinburgh: T. & T. Clark, 1996.

Canivez, Josephus M., editor. *Statuta capitulorum generalium ordinis Cisterciensis ab anno 1116 ad annum 1786*. 8 vols. Louvain: Bureaux de la Revue, 1933–41.

Casey, Michael. *Athirst for God: Spiritual Desire in Bernard of Clairvaux's Sermons on the Song of Songs*. Cistercian Studies 77. Kalamazoo, MI: Cistercian, 1988.

Classen, Albrecht. "Female Epistolary Literature from Antiquity to the Present: An Introduction." *Studia Neophilologia* 60 (1988) 3–13.

Constable, Giles. *Letters and Letter-Collections*. Turnhout: Brepols, 1976.

———. "Medieval Media: Mass Communication in the Making of Europe." Lecture delivered at the University of Southampton, Southampton, UK, March 14, 1972.

———. *The Reformation of the Twelfth Century*. Cambridge: Cambridge University Press, 1996.

Demacopoulos, George. *Five Models of Spiritual Direction in the Early Church*. Notre Dame: Notre Dame University Press, 2007.

Diers, Michaela. *Bernhard von Clairvaux: Elitäre Frömmigkeit und begnadetes Wirken*. Münster: Deutscher Taschenbuch, 1991.

Dumesnil, René. *Saint Bernard: Homme d' Action*. Paris: Desclée de Brouwer, 1934.

Evans, Gillian R. *Bernard of Clairvaux: Selected Works*. New York: Paulist, 1988.

Farkasfalvy, Denis. "The First Step in the Spiritual Life: Conversion." *Analecta Sacri Ordinis Cistercensis* 46 (1990) 65–84.

Fracheboud, M. André. "Je Suis La Chimèra de Mon Siècle: Le problème action-contemplation au cœur de saint Bernard." *Collectanea Ordinis Cisterciensium Reformatorum* 16 (1954) 45–52.

Gilson, Étienne. *The Mystical Theology of St. Bernard*. Translated by A. H. C. Downs. 1940. Reprint, Kalamazoo, MI: Cistercian, 1990.

Haskins, Charles H. *The Renaissance of the Twelfth Century*. Cambridge: Harvard University Press, 1927.

Irvine, Martin. *The Making of Textual Culture: 'Grammatica' and Literary Theory, 350–1100.* Cambridge Studies in Medieval Literature 19. Cambridge: Cambridge University Press, 1994.

James, Bruno Scott. *Saint Bernard of Clairvaux: An Essay in Biography.* New York: Harper, 1957.

Kereszty, Roch. "Relationship between Anthropology and Christology: St. Bernard, A Teacher for Our Age." *Analecta Sacri Ordinis Cistercensis* 46 (1990) 271–99.

Kienzle, Beverly M. "Tending the Lord's Vineyard: Cistercians, Rhetoric and Heresy, 1143–1229: Part 1: Bernard of Clairvaux, the 1143 Sermons and the 1145 Preaching Mission." *Heresis* 25 (1995) 29–61.

Knowles, David. *The Monastic Order in England: A History of Its Development from the Times of St. Dunstan to the Fourth Lateran Council, 940–1216.* 2nd ed. Cambridge: Cambridge University Press, 1963.

Krahmer, Shawn Madison. "Interpreting the Letters of Bernard of Clairvaux to Ermengarde, Countess of Brittany: The Twelfth-Century Context and the Language of Friendship." *Cistercian Studies* 27/3 (1992) 217–50.

Kristeller, Paul O. "Humanism and Scholasticism in the Italian Renaissance." *Byzantion* 17 (1944–45) 346–74.

Leclercq, Jean. *Bernard of Clairvaux and the Cistercian Spirit.* Cistercian Studies 16. Kalamazoo, MI: Cistercian, 1976.

———. "Lettres de S. Bernard: Introduction." *Recueil d'Etudes Sur Saint Bernard et Ses Écrites,* edited by Jean Leclercq, 37–61. Raccolta di Studi e Testi 182. Rome: Storia e Letteratura, 1992.

———. "Lettres de vocation à la vie monastique." *Studia Anselmiana* 37 (1955) 169–97.

———. *The Love of Learning and the Desire for God.* Translated by Catharine Misrahi. New York: Fordham, 1982.

———. *Monks on Marriage: A Twelfth-Century View.* New York: Seabury, 1982.

———. "Recherches sur la collection des épîtres de Saint Bernard." *Cahiers de civilization médiévale* 14 (1971) 205–19.

———. "Saint Bernard of Clairvaux and the Contemplative Community." *Cistercian Studies Quarterly* 7/2 (1972) 97–142.

———. "St. Bernard in our Times." In *St. Bernard of Clairvaux: Studies Commemorating the Eighth Centenary of his Canonization,* edited by M. Basil Pennington, 1–26. Cistercian Studies 28. Kalamazoo, MI: Cistercian, 1979.

———. "Toward a Sociological Interpretation of the Various Saint Bernards." In *Bernardus Magister,* edited by John R. Sommerfeldt, 19–33. Cistercian Studies 135. Kalamazoo, MI: Cistercian, 1992.

———. *Women and St. Bernard of Clairvaux.* Translated by Marie-Bernard Säid. Cistercian Studies 104. Kalamazoo, MI: Cistercian, 1989.

Lipkin, Joel. "The Entrance of the Cistercians into the Church Hierarchy, 1098–1227: The Bernardine Influence." In *The Chimæra of His Age: Studies on Bernard of Clairvaux,* edited by E. Rozanne Elder and John R. Sommerfeldt, Studies in Medieval Cistercian History 5, 62–73. Kalamazoo, MI: Cistercian, 1980.

Little, Edward F. "Relations between St. Bernard and Abelard before 1139." In *St. Bernard of Clairvaux: Studies Commemorating the Eighth Centenary of His Canonization,* Cistercian Studies 28, edited by M. Basil Pennington, 155–68. Kalamazoo, MI: Cistercian, 1979

Mahn, Jean-Berthold. *L'Ordre cistercien et son gouvernement des origines au milieu du xiiie siècle*. Paris: Les Belles Lettres, 1951.

McCaffrey, Hugh. "The Basics of Monastic Living in St. Bernard." *Cistercian Studies Quarterly* 25/3 (1990) 157–62.

McGinn, Bernard. "Freedom, Formation and Reformation: The Anthropological Roots of Saint Bernard's Spiritual Teaching." *Analecta Sacri Ordinis Cisterciensis* 46 (1990) 91–114.

———. *The Growth of Mysticism: Gregory the Great through the 12th Century*. New York: Crossroad, 2004.

McGuire, Brian P. *Friendship & Community: The Monastic Experience 350–1250*. Cistercian Studies 95. Kalamazoo, MI: Cistercian, 1988.

Murphy, James J. *Rhetoric in the Middle Ages: A History of Rhetorical Theory from St. Augustine to the Renaissance*. Berkeley: University of California Press, 1974.

Olivera, Bernardo. "Aspects of the Love of Neighbor in the Spiritual Doctrine of Saint Bernard (II)." *Cistercian Studies Quarterly* 26/3 (1991) 204–26.

Pennington, M. Basil. "Straight from the Shoulder of St. Bernard." *Cistercian Studies Quarterly* 4/3 (1969) 189–98.

———. "Three Stages of Spiritual Growth according to St. Bernard." *Studia Monastica* 11 (1969) 315–26.

———, editor. *St. Bernard of Clairvaux: Studies Commemorating the Eighth Centenary of His Canonization*. Cistercian Studies 28. Kalamazoo, MI: Cistercian, 1979.

Pfeifer, M. Michaela. "Klosterstreitigkeiten? Bernhard von Clairvaux vielschichtige Schlichtungsbriefe." *Cistercienser-Chronik* 110 (2003) 463–79.

Renna, Thomas. "The City in Early Cistercian Thought." *Citeaux* 34 (1983) 5–19.

Runciman, Steven. *A History of the Crusades*. Vol. 2, *The Kingdom of Jerusalem and the Frankish East, 1100–1187*. Cambridge: Cambridge University Press, 1999.

Smerillo, G. L. J. "*Caritas* in the Initial Letters of St. Bernard." In *Saint Bernard of Clairvaux: Studies Commemorating the Eighth Centenary of His Canonization*, edited by M. Basil Pennington. Cistecian Studies 28. Kalamazoo, MI: Cistercian, 1977.

Smith, Martin. "Contemplation and Action in the Pastoral Theology of St. Bernard." In *The Influence of St. Bernard: Anglican Essays with an Introduction by Jean Leclercq*, Fairacres Publication 60, edited by Benedicta Ward, 11–22. Oxford: S. L. G., 1976.

Sommerfeldt, John. *Bernard of Clairvaux: On the Life of the Mind*. Mahwah, NJ: Newman, 2004.

———. "Bernard of Clairvaux on Love and Marriage." *Cistercian Studies Quarterly* 30/2 (1995) 141–6.

———. *Bernard of Clairvaux: On the Spirituality of Relationship*. Mahwah, NJ: Newman, 2004.

———. "Vassals of the Lord and Ministers of God: The Role of the Governing Class in the Ecclesiology of Bernard of Clairvaux." *Cistercian Studies Quarterly* 29/1 (1994) 55–60.

Southern, R. W. *Western Society and the Church in the Middle Ages*. New York: Penguin, 1990.

St. Bernard of Clairvaux: The Story of His Life as Recorded in the Vita prima Bernardi by certain of His Contemporaries, William of St. Thierry, Arnold of Bonnevaux, Geoffrey and Philip of Clairvaux, and Odo of Deuil (Vita prima Bernardi). Translated by Geoffrey Webb and Adrian Walker. London: Mowbray, 1960.

Stiegman, Emero. "Bernard of Clairvaux, William of St. Thierry, The Victorines." In *The Medieval Theologians*, edited by G. R. Evans, 140–42. Cambridge: Blackwell, 2001.

Storrs, R. S. *Bernard of Clairvaux: The Times, the Man, and His Work. An Historical Study in Eight Lectures*. New York: Scribner, 1892.

Usāmah Ibn Munqidh. *An Arab-Syrian Gentleman and Warrior in the Period of the Crusades: Memoirs of Usāmah Ibn-Munqidh*. Translated by Philip K. Hatti. New York: Columbia University Press, 2000.

Warren, W. L. *Henry II*. Berkeley: University of California Press, 1977.

Williams, Watkin. "The Political Philosophy of Saint Bernard of Clairvaux." *Blackfriars* 24 (1944) 466–69.